Foreign Travelers in America
1810–1935

Foreign Travelers in America
1810–1935

Advisory Editors:

Arthur M. Schlesinger, Jr.
Eugene P. Moehring

AMERICA

M[organ] Philips Price

ARNO PRESS
A New York Times Company
New York—1974

Reprint Edition 1974 by Arno Press Inc.

Copyright © 1936 by George Allen & Unwin Ltd.
Reprinted by permission of
   George Allen & Unwin Ltd.

Reprinted from a copy in the State Historical
   Society of Wisconsin Library

FOREIGN TRAVELERS IN AMERICA, 1810-1935
ISBN for complete set: 0-405-05440-8
See last pages of this volume for titles.

Manufactured in the United States of America

Library of Congress Cataloging in Publication Data

Price, Morgan Philips, 1885-
   America.

   (Foreign travelers in America, 1810-1935)
   Reprint of the 1936 ed. published by G. Allen &
Unwin, London, under title: America after sixty years:
the travel diaries of two generations of Englishmen.
   CONTENTS: pt. 1. 1869: Captain W. E. Price's
American journey.--pt. 2. 1878: Major and Mrs. Price's
American tour.--pt. 3. Impressions of America under
the New Deal.
   1. United States--Description and travel. 2. Unit-
ed States--Social and conditions. I. Price, William
Edwin, 1841-1886. II. Price, Margaret (Philips)
d. 1911. III. Title. IV. Series.
E169.P89 1974   917.3'04'808   73-13146
ISBN 0-405-05470-X

AMERICA AFTER SIXTY YEARS

The Travel Diaries of
Two Generations of Englishmen

THE AUTHORS

M. PHILIPS PRICE, M.P.
1935

CAPT. W. E. PRICE, M.P.
1869

AMERICA
AFTER SIXTY YEARS

The Travel Diaries
of
Two Generations of Englishmen

by

M. PHILIPS PRICE
M.P., M.A., F.R.G.S.

LONDON
GEORGE ALLEN & UNWIN LTD
MUSEUM STREET

FIRST PUBLISHED IN 1936

PRINTED IN GREAT BRITAIN BY
UNWIN BROTHERS LTD., WOKING

PREFACE

GOOD fortune has enabled me, in the following pages, to do something which but few authors can have had the opportunity of doing: I have published my parents' diaries of travel in the United States of America, and have followed them with a diary of my own, which describes how I covered the same ground sixty years later.

My father, Captain W. E. Price, after he had been elected to Parliament in 1868, made his first journey on the American continent during a Parliamentary recess. Young public men in England in those days were interested by the reports of what was happening across the Atlantic, for about this time the pioneering boom in the West was at its height. My family, moreover, had commercial interests in North America, mainly in timber—in the Eastern States and Canada—and railways. So, after attending to certain business affairs in Canada, my father set off across the continent with three companions, who like him were members of the House of Commons. The Civil War had not long been over, so that, apart from business and sight-seeing, they were concerned to note the political repercussions of that titanic contest. One of my father's companions was Sir Michael Hicks-Beach, later Lord St. Aldwyn. Another was John Frederick Cheetham, a Lancashire mill-owner, and Liberal M.P. for Stalybridge. The third was Lord Garlies, Conservative M.P. for Wigtonshire, and son of the Earl of Galloway, who later succeeded to his father's title.

My father's diaries throw side-lights on a number of half-forgotten topics which are nevertheless of no small interest, even at this remove of time: such as the under-currents of Canadian politics in the 60's, life in Chicago just before the great fire, and the journey from ocean to ocean in one of the first Transcontinental expresses. The Union Pacific had linked up with the Southern Pacific, at Promontory Creek in Utah, only a few months earlier, so that my father and his friends must have been in one of the first ten or twelve weekly express trains to cross the continent. The diary then records an interesting journey to the Yosemite Valley, not many years after its first discovery by pioneer ranchers. The description of a visit to Salt Lake City shows how acute the Mormon question was at this period. Finally, the pages dealing with a visit to the Southern States are of especial interest, as only four years had elapsed since the close of the Civil War, and Reconstruction was at its height. One could wish that this part of the diary had been a little fuller.

Nine years later my father paid a second visit to the United States, this time on his honeymoon with my mother. He was still a Member of Parliament, and also Major in the Gloucestershire Militia. He traversed some of the ground of his previous trip, and noted the various changes that had taken place. I have selected extracts from both my father's and my mother's letters home on this occasion. But the interesting feature of this part of the diaries is the remarkable journey which they made—unique, I should say, for a honeymoon—into the frontier districts of New Mexico in a United States army ambulance! A stroke of luck brought my parents into touch with General Sherman, who at this time was Commander-in-Chief of the United States Army. He was making a tour of inspection of the New Mexico garrisons, and supervising operations against the Indians, then a source of trouble to the authorities. My father evidently had much in common with General Sherman, and, although the subject of his conversations with the General are not dealt with in any detail in the diaries, I remember my mother telling me how greatly my father valued his passing acquaintance with the great man, and in what high esteem he held him, not only as a soldier, but also as a shrewd observer of human nature. A portrait of the General, signed by himself and given to my father, is still in my possession.

Fifty-six years later my wife and I visited the United States, and Part III of this book is based on my diary and the rough notes made during the journey. We decided to follow as closely as possible the routes taken by my parents in 1869 and 1878. Again we noted the great change that had come over America in the interval, paying special attention to the social and economic problems before the country. Having seen Russia during the Revolution, in 1917 and 1918, I wanted to see how the United States, with its very different traditions and history, was facing the crisis of an economic collapse, which Russia had experienced fifteen years earlier. Both countries were vast continents with endless resources behind them; but one was developed, and the other undeveloped; one was a democracy while the other had always been despotically governed.

My wife and I entered the United States after the New Deal had been in operation for eighteen months. As an agriculturalist I was especially eager to study the results of the A.A.A. programme in the Middle West—which explains why we spent so much time there—in the Far West, and in the Southern States.

It was fortunate that our visit coincided with the November elections of 1934—and it should be remembered that the record of this journey must be read in the light of the situation existing in the country in the autumn of that year. Much has happened since, and not least, the fateful decision of the United States Supreme Court on the New Deal in May 1935. This part of the diary is a pen-picture

of the autumn and early winter of 1934, and makes no
pretence at being other than topical.

From these pages the reader will gather my feelings as to
the need of the peoples of the British and American Commonwealths to understand each other's problems in the modern
world. Central Europe is slowly drifting into barbarism,
and Russia, though a great and hopeful social experiment, is
no example of methods for the Anglo-Saxon worlds to
follow, since its political and cultural traditions are not ours.
It remains for the people of the British and American
Commonwealths to show the world that they can carry
through great and critical reforms and at the same time
retain their ancient political liberties. Our changed circumstances, so different from those of my father's days, for he
left England and saw the United States when Victorian
prosperity and Western pioneering were at their height,
were constantly before me as I crossed the continent, nearly
sixty years later.

M. PHILIPS PRICE

THE GROVE, TAYNTON, NR. GLOUCESTER.
September 1935.

CONTENTS

ILLUSTRATIONS

Part One

1869

CAPTAIN W. E. PRICE'S
AMERICAN JOURNEY

I have been so over head and ears in gaiety for the last week that I have had no time at all to write. My last letter was from Montreal, on Thursday, September 30th, just as we were leaving for Kingston. We had taken a trip to Burlington in Vermont, gone over Lake Champlain in a special steamer placed at our disposal, visited the Eau Sauble Chasru in the lower range of the Adironack, and spent a day with a Yankee gentleman, Colonel Cannon.

I was exceedingly pleased with him, as he was an example of a real Yankee gentleman—a true American and a staunch Republican—and yet he is a man of very advanced and independent views, seeing the faults of his own Government, and fully appreciating the good points of our Constitution. He is also a distinguished soldier, having previously served in the United States Army, and he then re-entered the service and fought through the whole war.

He has a charming country residence near Burlington. His daughters were thorough Americans, but very lady-like —though they abused soundly the taste in dress of English ladies and the dancing of English gentlemen. They admired the horsemanship of English ladies, and abused the Americans for their want of energy.

We left Montreal on Friday, October 1st, in a "wild cat" train—i.e., a special, with movements as erratic as those of a wild cat. The Directors' car was a house in itself, with four bedrooms, drawing-room and anteroom, and attached to it was another for the suite, containing a sort of kitchen, &c. We travelled over the line to Kingston, stopping at every place of interest, either from its scenery or its importance as connected with Grand Trunk.

We stayed at Kingston for the night, and were fed in the

most *recherché* manner by an old Frenchman, named Beaufort, who has leased all the Grand Trunk refreshment-rooms. M. Beaufort gave us the most splendid banquet he could accomplish, and he being a Frenchman, his efforts were successful. I, unfortunately, was suffering from the effects of drinking Ottawa water, which is a rank poison, owing to the sulphate of lime which it contains. Being very thirsty one day I drank a large quantity, and had to take about fifty drops of chlorodyne at various times to recover from the effects.

Saturday we continued our journey to Toronto, and reached it at four the same evening. Toronto was in a state of feverish loyalty, which manifested itself in triumphal arches, decorations, fireworks, and innumerable British flags. The Canadians are in a terrible state on account of the belief which they entertain that the English Liberal party want to hand them over to America. They are, without exaggeration, perfectly frantic at the idea of annexation, or independence, which means annexation. Hence the degree of loyalty with which Prince Arthur is received everywhere in Canada. Poor wretch! He has a hard time of it, and no doubt curses the Liberals for the ebullition of feeling which they have called forth. On Saturday night I went to see the prizes presented to the Toronto Militia, as fine a body of men as I could wish to see, but not so well drilled as the South Gloucesters. They would whip the Yankees into fits, though, at the rate of two to one, if properly officered.

On Sunday I spent the whole day with a Toronto man, to whom I was introduced, and who took me out to his farm in the country, where I had a long talk about Canadian farming with his Scotch bailiff. I met a great number of Canadians at dinner, who pursued me like swallows after a hawk, because I was an English M.P., my arrival being duly chronicled in all the evening papers two hours after I got to Toronto. I received immense hospitality from all of them—

going I think to four houses that evening to smoke a cigar and talk, and go through the farce of eating supper, which so far as I was concerned consisted of a glass of champagne. I endeavoured to convince all my entertainers that I was not in favour of annexation, but only of not opposing the Canadians if they wished it; and I assured them that I was quite convinced that the feeling was against it.

I had a great deal of talk about Canadian politics during my stay in Toronto and elsewhere, and have, I think, got a tolerably clear idea on the subject. On Monday I went over the University of Toronto and the Law Courts—both magnificent buildings, and the former a very beautiful specimen of Norman Gothic—richly decorated with grotesque carvings, and built of fine grey sandstone from Ohio. I have never seen a building which pleased me so much. But the institution is behind the age, though making efforts to keep up with it. It has only just succeeded in emancipating itself from the Church of England, and is still really under its influence. I dined afterwards with a large company of Canadians, chiefly legal men, and enjoyed myself much, as I had a fine opportunity to hear all they had to say—and as most of them were Judges, Chief Justices, &c., &c., what I heard was upon good authority.

I went to the Ball afterwards, given by the citizens of Toronto to Prince Arthur. Of course, all our party received invitations. I danced with a few Canadian ladies. Then I joined various knots of politicians, and went into Canadian politics. The Prince had a special supper for himself and suite, which of course was far superior to the supper served out to those who sat below the salt. I was invited down with a select party to taste it before it was put on the table, and fully appreciated the *perdrix aux truffes* and *Roederer Carte Blanche*—very dry! I went to bed about four, and was up at eight, to go in a special train to Weston, there to witness

19

the ceremony of cutting the first sod of the Toronto–Grey and Bruce railway. We had a luncheon provided, and the ceremony was interesting only on account of the enthusiasm of the people for the Prince. Two country girls—young ladies I suppose they called themselves—got so excited that they rushed up and grasped the Prince's hand just as he was composing his features to be photographed. He was rather disconcerted at this sudden attack, but took it good humouredly, though he blushed to his eyes.

I chaffed the girls afterwards, as I happened to sit next to them at the luncheon, and one of them said: "He is a duck and a darling—I wouldn't go away without shaking hands!" I said: "You ought to have kissed him," to which she replied—"Oh, I wish he would let me!"

I attended two luncheons after this—one given to Mr. Porter by the Grand Trunk people, and the other to the Governor-General by the Mayor and Council of Toronto. At the latter I was to have responded to the toast of the "English House of Commons," but the time passed so quickly that it was impossible to get through the toasts.— I was also presented to the Governor-General at the Levée which he held. My costume was a black morning coat and a round hat, &c. Rather a strange costume for a Levée held by Her Majesty's Representative, according to English notions, but a very sensible alteration, I think. That evening I went to a Grand Ball given by McPherson—a rich Canadian merchant and a Senator. Prince Arthur and all the great men of the Dominion were there, and everybody who was anybody, and a good many who were not. I never saw a finer thing—the room built on purpose for dancing—acres of glass conservatory thrown open—grounds lighted up by Chinese lanterns—in fact, you must imagine it, for I have no time to describe it. I danced only with Kate and Blanche, for I was tired.

I have said nothing about our party. Bridges, the Managing Director of the Grand Trunk—Hickson, the second in command—Mr. Richard Potter,[1] Kate,[2] Blanche and myself, have generally been together. Beach[3] went off to Ottawa, and my friend Cheetham also went there, without, however, knowing Beach had gone, and they reached Toronto only on Tuesday, in time for the Ball. On Wednesday we spent the whole day going over the University, Common Schools and Normal Schools with Professor Wilson, and we got lots of books, reports, &c., to post us up in the Canadian Education question. Beach does not like the system, but I do, and am convinced that the Act would apply well to England.

I dined that night with the Hon. Geo. Brown, a former member of the Government, but now in the cold shade of Opposition; a Canadian Radical, and loyal to us, and a clever and honest but impracticable man. He hates the Grand Trunk, so he and Potter don't hit it off, but the fact is that the Grand Trunk is a great political machine in Canada, and it ought not to be.

On Thursday we came on to Niagara Falls, that is, Mrs. Bridges, Kate, Blanche, Beach, Cheetham and myself; Mr. Potter and Bridges remaining behind to go over some branch lines. We spent two hours at Hamilton, a large and flourishing town on Lake Ontario, and ascended a fine hill, which gave a splendid view of the country, and was interesting to me geologically.

Our first impressions of the Falls were not satisfactory. The moon was young and the night dark, and the Falls lost in grandeur. Early next morning we turned out and visited the American side first, went over to Goat Island, down to

[1] Chairman of the Grand Trunk.
[2] Daughter of Richard Potter. She later married Lord Courtney, Liberal publicist and politician.
[3] Sir Michael Hicks-Beach, later Lord St. Aldwyn.

the Cave of the Winds, under a part of the American falls, and to all the other parts of interest. Today we have been doing (and the others are still doing) the Canadian side and the Horse-Shoe Falls.

The ladies, Beach, and Cheetham have lost their senses, I think. They stand and gaze for hours. I am tired of the whole thing, and although impressed with the natural beauty of the scenery I see in it too immediately before me merely the working of the most ordinary natural laws, and the only feeling of grandeur which is present to my mind is the vast immensity of time which has elapsed since the channel of the Niagara river has been hollowed out. I have never seen a natural phenomenon which shows so clearly the vastness of geological time as Niagara Falls. This, of course, is appreciated only by a geologist, and I have spent all the morning trying to unravel the history of the surrounding country—and I think successfully. Of course, everyone laughs at me, and pities my apparent want of feeling and appreciation of the sublime spectacle, &c. But it is not a high order of intellect which prompts a man to stand gazing at the Falls for hours, in a trance or dream which has no meaning and can't be analysed. A grand natural pheno-menon, and very interesting from a geological point of view, but as an object of real grandeur not in the least degree comparable to a storm at sea, or wild mountain scenery. Its causes are too evident, while the causes of the others are too remote. There is no mystery about Niagara, not even the mystery of a geological problem. At first sight the enormous mass of water washing over the limestone cliff is very grand, but it soon becomes wearisome. It is noisy and blustering, and palls on both eye and ear.

Tonight Beach, Cheetham and myself leave at 12 a.m. for Detroit, spend Sunday (tomorrow) there, and go on Monday to Ann Arbor in Michigan, to see the University of Michigan, celebrated for being the exponent of a new theory, which is really a very old one, of University education, i.e., no competition. There is much to be said for it, and I believe it is a success.

We have beautiful weather, real Indian summer with all the most glorious tints of autumn, from deep scarlet and purple to grey and silver. The weather, however, has been very variable. Bitterly cold one day, wet the next, and warm the next after that. The climate of Canada is very changeable, but once the Indian summer sets in it lasts for a fortnight, and glorious weather it is, too good to be wasted in pottering about Niagara.

We arrived here, the most extreme Western City, this morning at eight o'clock, and we stay here till Tuesday morning, when we start for San Francisco, arriving there on Friday evening. We were four days at Chicago, and were well pleased with it. It is the most flourishing place on the Western side of America, and yet thirty-five years ago it had a population of about 100 people, grouped around a small American outpost called Dearborn Fort. The most remarkable thing to see in Chicago is the way they move houses. All the Western cities, and indeed most American cities, are built to a great extent of wood. The large stores and public buildings, of course, are of stone, but most of the private residences are wooden, and are sometimes faced with stone.

Chicago is situated on Lake Michigan, and lies low, and a few years ago they decided to raise the whole town bodily. This they are doing by getting under the foundations and raising up each house by screw-jacks. One often notices that the pavement at the side of the houses is two or three feet or more above the road level, showing how the houses have been pushed up. Then the wooden houses are frequently dug up and carried off to another site. Leases run out, and people buy land in other places, and transport their houses, often with their families indoors, to the new site. I saw one in transit, with the people inside, mounted on rollers, and being dragged along slowly by windlasses worked by horses.

I visited the stockyards on Wednesday, and saw some fine specimens of Western cattle. Chicago is the great central depôt for stock of all kinds, but chiefly for cattle and pigs. They slaughter thousands, and for pigs they have a machine which the pig enters, and before his last squeal dies away he comes out pork ready for shipment! Thousands of cattle too are shipped to the Eastern cities, bred in Missouri, Texas and the West generally. The Texans have horns seven feet across, the largest I ever saw, as large as those of the Assam buffalo, and they are half wild and very savage. The ordinary Western cattle, however, attain the largest size. I stood up by a fat steer, and could just reach his withers, by standing on tiptoe, with the tips of my fingers. He was immensely fat, and weighed, I was told, 4,000 lb., and they sometimes run to 6,000 lb. weight.

I saw the same day a trotting race, having received a complimentary invitation to be present. I never saw such trotting in my life. A mile in 2′ 29″! It has been done in 2′ 18″. The driver sits on a sort of skeleton gig, very light, and used only for racing purposes. The Americans get immensely excited over these races, and all attempts of the police to restrain them are ineffectual. On Thursday we went to Joliet, about forty miles away, to see the State Penitentiary. This is a prison where all who are sentenced for twelve months or upwards are sent. The establishment is self-supporting, every prisoner having to work at some regular trade. The prison is very large, and contains about 1,500 prisoners, with workshops for every class of industry— carriage-building, iron-founding, saddle-making, tailoring, shoe-making, chair-making, agricultural implement-making, carpentering, weaving, stone-cutting; everything is made within the prison walls, and each man has to learn a trade if he does not already belong to one. There are magnificent quarries of freestone close at hand, and gangs are sent out every day to work these, the men being chiefly those who belong to no trade, gentlemen, &c., or those who have short sentences. Contracts are taken by the Prison authorities, though the ordinary goods are not sold cheaper than at the stores, so as not to disturb the trade. A balance remains every year to the credit of the State after paying all expenses, so the State, instead of being taxed for the support of its prisoners, actually makes a profit out of them. We in England shall have to come to some arrangement of this kind, as the working of the new "Habitual Criminals Act" will tend to fill our jails with men who will spend the greater part of their lives there, and the expense will be enormous.

The curious thing in the Illinois Penitentiary is that the prisoners are made so comfortable. They work together, are allowed to talk, are provided with tobacco by the State, have meat twice a day, are encouraged to read, have a candle in their cells every night, and, when well behaved, are allowed to work overtime and earn money, which they spend on books. I saw several cells with good collections of books, including Shakespeare and Milton, Macaulay, &c. These belong chiefly to men under sentence for life.

Capital punishment is forbidden in the State by statute, though the Warden thought they would have to revert to it again. The lash is forbidden, and discipline is maintained by moral influence, the only punishment being solitary confinement in dark cells. I have every reason to believe that this succeeds, and the Warden says he has very little difficulty in maintaining order, except occasionally with Irishmen. We were hospitably received by the officials, and had supper with the Warden. We were waited upon by convicts—all the work indoors, as well as the cooking, baking, slaughtering and gardening, being done by the convicts.

We left Chicago yesterday morning, having secured sleeping-berths in a Pullman Car. When we had covered about thirty miles of our journey one of the wheels was discovered to be on fire, and was blazing brilliantly. The friction had set fire to the oil in the wheel-box. It took us half an hour to put it out. Soon after proceeding on our journey, however, another wheel was discovered to be on fire, and so it went on, with wheel after wheel, until at last they had to leave the sleeping-car behind, and we were bundled into another ordinary car. We were very indignant, of course, but I always treat these things philosophically when travelling and my equanimity was rewarded, for at Cedar Rapids, where we arrived at 8 p.m., we found another Pullman Car, and so got our beds for the night. We did not succeed, however, in getting any sleep, for the late heavy floods had swept away the ballast, and the line was barely safe to travel on. The jolting was fearful, and at times we seemed to be altogether in the air. On venturing a mild remark to the conductor—who, by the way, like all American conductors, was a very good fellow—he said he guessed that was nothing compared to what it would be about twelve o'clock. And as the car was the worst on the line—only kept for emergencies—he reckoned it might not keep the track; and how it did keep it, in spite of every inducement to leave it, was a mystery to me.

Soon after leaving Chicago we crossed the Mississippi, at Fulton in Iowa State, and then we got into real prairie land. Farms here and there, and crops of Indian corn, but generally wide rolling prairie, swelling into bluffs, intersected by marshy streams and teeming with wild fowl, quails and prairie grouse. As we neared this place it grew wilder and wilder, until we saw in the distance, at daybreak this morning, some high bluffs rising to westward. These were Council Bluffs, situated on the Iowa side of the Missouri, and so called from some conference with the Indians held there a few years ago. Crossing the Missouri by ferry, we got into Nebraska, a new State, just admitted, and its capital, Omaha City, where we now are. Every collection of tents and wooden houses is called a city in the West, but this is a large place for such a city, although the population is a floating one, and the majority of the houses are drinking and gambling places.

The population are rough Western men, miners from Virginia City and Carson in Nevada or Colorado—loafers, thieves, *et hoc genus omne*. Still, they are quiet enough, and don't take pot shots at one's hat to test their revolvers. They are rough good-natured fellows, offended if you don't take a drink with them, and, except the thieves and loafers, good citizens.

I shall not write again, probably, until I reach California next Friday or Saturday.

YOSEMITE VALLEY,
SIERRA NEVADA MTS., CALIFORNIA.
Monday, November 1, 1869.

On Saturday the 16th we left for Omaha, twenty-four hours distant, having obtained passes over the line, our only expenses being the extra charge for berths and for food on the way. With us on the train were two English snobs, whose luggage was marked "Hon. Algar" and "Hon. Snellie." They were on a shooting expedition; one of them had a gun or rifle done up in newspaper, and the other remarked to my companion that he had one hundred round of ball cartridge, which he thought would last for the first few days.

They were most offensive in their snobbishness, and Beach and I were very angry to think that such specimens of English nobility should show themselves in America. We explained everywhere that we did not recognize them, and believed them to be snobs.—We had various adventures on the journey; our carriage wheels caught fire, and we had to clear out, as I think I mentioned in a former letter.

On Sunday, October 17th, we reached Omaha, which may be called a frontier city between civilization, and the Western prairies. The weather was most bitter, a cold North wind blowing, and snow threatening. We had a horrid bad hotel to stay in, and spent two very unpleasant days.

On Tuesday the 19th, Lord Garlies joined us at breakfast-time, and at 10 a.m. we all four started on our expedition to San Francisco, 1,900 miles over the Rocky Mountains, crossing the Grand Plateau at Sherman, at a height of 8,000 feet, and the Salt Lake Desert (all alkali and sage-bush) and the Sierra Nevadas—by a pass 7,500 feet above sea-level—and then descending the beautiful Western slopes into California. Our train was the first of a series of weekly expresses which run the distance from Omaha in three and a half days instead of four and a half, and are fitted up with sleeping- and commissary-cars. The train is called the Pullman Palace Car Express. There are no ordinary cars, but only magnificently fitted sleeping-cars, converted into drawing-rooms in the daytime, and in one of them a fine harmonium or organ, as they call it, with lots of stops, and of capital tone.

The dining-car accommodated twenty people at a time. We had meals on board, and fared first rate. Of course, the charge for this train is very high. We endeavoured to get passes, but failed, and paid our fares: 168 dollars (about £33). A great number of passengers had taken places from New York, but an accident delayed them all to the east of Chicago, so we started on Tuesday with only twelve on board; much to our advantage, I can assure you. The first day was uninteresting, the route lying along the Platte River, over dreary boundless prairie, passing every now and then some wood and water station carefully guarded by a detachment of United States troops. The Sioux and Cheyenne Indians here are very troublesome, and are always plundering and murdering when they get a chance. At Plum Creek[1] I had a talk with the officer in charge, who told me he had just returned from an expedition; he had killed nine buffalo and two Indians, and had lost one man wounded. The buffalo and the Indians seemed to be both in the same category—i.e., game. But he explained that these were Indians of a hostile tribe, and they killed them whenever they met them. At Medicine Boy[2] we heard of a foray which had just taken place. A man in charge of the line, with his wife and two children, was attacked by Indians, and his wife was shot in the arm. The husband bagged only one Indian, but the

[1] About 220 miles West-south-west of Omaha in Nebraska.
[2] On Laramie Plains.

troops were after them, and I hope have given a good account of themselves. We are going to stay with them at Fort Laramie on our return, so perhaps we shall get a full report.

Early on Wednesday the 20th we woke up to find the ground covered with snow, on either side the rolling prairie, as white as possible, and dotted with antelope, prairie dogs, wolves and coyotes. The antelope were very numerous, but we saw no buffalo as it was too late in the season. We had been gradually ascending all night, and were then at an altitude of 5,000 feet, although the ground seemed quite level, and no Rocky Mountains were in sight. At ten we reached Cheyenne City, a dirty settlement of wooden houses and tents, every other one of them a drinking place or gambling house, and at twelve we passed the highest point of the Rocky Mountain route—Sherman,[1] 8,000 feet high—without being conscious of having ascended at all since we started. The fact is that the Rocky Mountains rise so gradually from the East that they are inappreciable, but once you are past what they call the Divide you find yourself at once in a wild rocky desert that fully warrants the name. North and South of the railway—that is, in Colorado southwards, and in British territory northwards—the slope is less gradual, but the Platte prairies are really the Eastern slopes of that part of the Rockies. The descent from Sherman is about 1,000 feet, and then we reached the great plateau, beginning with the Laramie[2] plains, about fifty miles long and 6,000 feet above sea-level, affording capital pasturage.

At Laramie City a Colonel Henderson and a Dr. Latham got in, and travelled with us for a couple of hours, having learned by telegraph that we were coming. Dr. Latham is Medical Officer in charge of the railway and Colonel Hender-

[1] About fifty miles West of Cheyenne on Wyoming-Colorado State line.
[2] A little to the West of Sherman.

son commands the troops. Latham is a geologist, and we at once liquored *à l'Américain* and were soon deep in scientific problems. Garlies discussed on military subjects with Henderson, and we received a most pressing invitation to spend a few days with them on our return, which Garlies and I are going to do. They will provide us with weapons, and we are to have a grand hunt after elk, &c., with strict injunctions to shoot any stray Indians who may seem disposed to fancy the colour of our hair. I guess he will find mighty little on my head, as it is nearly all cut off to save me the trouble of brushing it.

Thursday 31st. Passed the various ridges of the Rocky Mountains on Wednesday evening and sighted the Rattlesnake Mountains and the Wasatch Range, when we got up, and were much pleased with the grand scenery, the very absence of wildness and desolation—The Echo Cañon, Weber's Cañon, and the Deirligate Cañon were especially fine: great gorges scooped out of the solid rock by the rivers and torrents which had been working at it for innumerable years, cutting through the softer strata, and leaving the harder in all sorts of fantastic shapes. Past Weber's Cañon we emerged upon a plain dotted with wooden houses and farms (or ranches, as they are called here), and found that we were amongst the Mormons. We saw at once that we had returned to civilization—troops of horses, herds of cattle and flocks of sheep on the plains and mountain-sides, and near the rivers patches of corn, wheat and barley—the latter stacked, the former ready to cut—all showed that Mormon energy was at work, and that religion, which had tried its hand at most things, had at last turned its attention to one subject, and achieved a complete success in it—agriculture to wit—for the Mormons say that the first precept of their religion is to cultivate the soil—turn barren rock into a garden—and avoid all argument and strife except that of the spade.

SCENES IN THE FAR WEST, 1869

PASSENGER TRAIN ON THE CENTRAL PACIFIC RAILWAY

EMIGRANT CAMP IN THE ROCKY MOUNTAINS

SCENES IN THE FAR WEST, 1869

PIONEER TOWN, CISCO, UTAH

PIONEER TEAMS IN THE ROCKY MOUNTAINS

In obedience to this article of their faith the Mormons have certainly achieved a grand success. They are peaceful, industrious and contented, according to all the accounts of their critics and visitors, but I fear the Americans won't let them alone, and that an awkward time is in store for them. New England has it in her heart to preach a crusade, but it will be to her lasting disgrace if she endeavours to drive out the Mormons on account of their faith. I fear there are some who have the same feelings as the early Puritans, and Artemus Ward speaks of those "who fled from the intolerance of their native land to a new country where they might enjoy in peace their own religion and prevent everyone else from enjoying theirs."

I am speaking of the Mormons now because everybody is full of the Mormon question, and I have heard it much discussed. You will hear more about it in another week, when I hope to be in Salt Lake City, when I can form my own opinion of them.

Soon after leaving Weber's Plains we passed the Devil's Gate and emerged upon the great Salt Lake Plain—a wide, dreary plain stretching for hundreds of miles East, West, North and South, and connecting with similar plains in Colorado to the South, and running up to Montana and Idaho Territory to the North. This vast plain, one hollow of which is occupied by the Great Salt Lake, is known as the Great American Desert. It consists of clay and sand impregnated with alkali, containing pools of brine, and often incrusted with salt, and producing nothing but sage-bush and stunted junipers. The picture is one of intense desolation, and occasional wooden crosses, marking the graves of the unfortunate pioneers of the desert, and the Salt Lake pilgrims, who died by the score when crossing this inhospitable region, by no means added to the cheerfulness of the scene.

The wayside was literally strewn with the bones of cattle and horses, showing how badly it fared with them as well as with human beings. For five hours we traversed this desert, and then reached Promontory City,[1] where the Union Pacific ends and the Central Pacific begins. The city consists of thirty wooden houses and tents on one side of the line, every one of which is a gambling house, containing Faro and Monte tables, where passengers are invited in, to be plundered or shot if they refuse to pay. There is absolutely no law in the desert, and every man in Promontory who is not a railway official or passenger is a murderer and ruffian of the worst kind. Luckily the thirty houses don't contain many, but they come and go. About six houses on the other side, inhabited by railway officials, complete the so-called "City." Their inmates keep to their own side, and hold no communication with the people on the other. Garlies and I went into one of the gambling saloons and looked about us, but we soon made tracks, and were not complimented on our somewhat hasty retreat.

At nightfall we entered Nevada Territory, escaping from the desert to a more congenial soil and climate. Here for the first time we saw groups of Chinese employed as labourers on the line. They were smiling, good-tempered fellows, as always, much amused when I "chin-chin'd" them and chaffed them in their own language.

Friday 22nd.—Got up early, as the scenery was changing, and assuming quite a new character. After leaving the alkali flats the previous evening we crossed the Toano Range into the Humboldt Valley,[2] up the Humboldt River, over the Red Range into the Truckee River valley. Both these rivers lose themselves in what are called "sinks." They disappear into the ground, their exit from the surface being

[1] North of Great Salt Lake and across the Nevada–Utah line.
[2] In North-east Nevada.

34

marked by a lake in the spring, and, I imagine, a marsh at all other seasons, as the country is scantily provided with water, and no great quantity of rain falls. We arrived at Truckee about 9 a.m. on Friday, and then commenced the ascent of Summit Pass. Snow was lying thickly on the ground and the gradient was very steep. Consequently we moved very slowly, winding up the hills and enjoying the scenery. The hills were covered with vegetation—pines of various kinds, and oaks and other trees which I could not distinguish.

This part of the line is the most difficult to keep open, as much snow lies in the winter, and drifts over the track. Avalanches too are frequent in the spring. To guard against them they have built sheds over the lines for thirty miles, beginning about ten miles from Truckee and fifteen from the highest point (7,500 feet), known as "Summit," and extending to a settlement called Culfax on the other side.

After entering the snowsheds one catches only occasional glimpses of the scenery, but the train stops frequently, and one can get out every five miles and look out from the sheds over the valleys below. The American trains are very different from the English. The cars are very long, holding fifty people, and the connecting gangways enable you to move about over the whole length of the train. What a benighted set of railway directors we have in England! There is no reason why we should not adopt the American system. Accidents are rarer in America than at home, so our system cannot be retained on the ground of safety—nor on the ground of pace, for fifty miles an hour is often done on the Pacific. But I am digressing for the pleasure of abusing our railway directors, the Midland especially![1]

About five miles to the east of Summit the train stopped

[1] His father was Chairman of the Midland Railway in Great Britain.—M. P. P.

for water, and we all got out. I was some distance ahead, and quite overlooked the fact that the sheds were supported by uprights at intervals of about six feet, and close to the line of rails. As the train came up it had gained sufficient speed to render it impossible for me to jump on to the steps without running the risk of being carried against the next upright. Each carriage passed me in succession (four altogether), and my only chance lay in catching the gangway at the end of the last car, but the train was travelling too fast, and I missed it. The cord which communicated with the engine-driver was unhitched, as this was a sort of special train, and before the driver could be warned the train was over the summit, and going down the gradient at forty or fifty miles an hour. They were twenty miles away before they were able to stop, so they concluded to go on and leave me to my own devices, since the conductor said that it was dangerous to go back—for reasons which soon became evident to me. I was quite happy in my misfortune, walked calmly over the summit, and made up my mind to take things leisurely and trust to chance.

After walking some distance, during which time a freight train passed me, I came to a signal station, and was informed that an emigrant train was coming up behind, and into that I got, my ticket being good for any train and at any time, as all tickets in America are, and as they ought to be in England. I shall certainly vote for putting our railways under State control!—The emigrant train had been seven days doing what we had done in two days, so my onward progress that day was slow. Most of the time we went on for half an hour, and then stopped for half an hour, and so on. We stopped for a long time at Culfax, Alta, Goldrun, Dutch Flat and Rocklands, all gold-mining districts, now nearly worked out, but bearing the marks of many years of hard work about them. The clay and gravel had all been dug away and washed, and the mountains were scarped from summit to base. These diggings are now worked chiefly by Chinamen. The scenery was very grand down the Western slopes, the pine-covered slopes of the Sierras, after the desert, being very pleasant to our eyes, wearied by the monotony of the plains and the alkali flats. I reached Sacramento at noon, having taken nothing since morning but an apple, a hard biscuit given me by an emigrant, and a glass of brandy. I had three dollars in paper in my pocket, and some gold and silver in the currency of California, and as you may imagine, I was not very clear as to where I could get a lodging and dinner for that sum, which amounted only to two dollars in gold.

Luckily I met a civil American (but they are all civil in this country) who at once offered me his purse, not knowing in the least who I was. I took three dollars, and went to a hotel, and enjoyed a pretty fair dinner. I had telegraphed to my companions early that morning, soon after I lost them, so my luggage was taken care of, and next morning I went on to San Francisco by passenger train, and joined my friends at lunch-time, none the worse for my adventure. Upon leaving Sacramento you get at once into the Californian Plain or Basin, which lies between the foothills of the Sierra and the Coast Range of mountains. The country is extremely fertile, tolerably well settled and cultivated, and grows great quantities of corn. The climate is perfection—not too hot, never very cold—a fresh breeze every day at twelve. It is the grandest climate in the world, healthy in the extreme, and though dreamy and soft, it is never enervating, thanks to the fresh sea-breeze coming in through the Golden Gate. Men who leave California generally come back. Ten years there makes them feel that they cannot live in any other climate; yet they are a sturdy, big-framed people, as vigorous as the best of the Anglo Saxon race.

San Francisco is a large city of 140,000 inhabitants, 25,000 of whom are Chinamen. The city has not, as I expected, a Spanish appearance. It has a genuine Anglo-America look, the principal English feature being, I think, the aspect of the inhabitants. We spent a very pleasant time there, receiving much hospitality, especially from Mr. Balston, a banker who took us out to his house and kept us there all day. He has built a perfect palace, with every new improvement, a picture-gallery, a music-room, and thirty or forty bedrooms, and he generally has the house full. His wife was a very nice person who had lived some time in Europe. He drove us all round the country, and showed us the best of the gardens and residences of the rich San Francisco merchants. The gardens are splendid, flowers of every hue growing most luxuriant, and humming-birds flying about, making quite a tropical scene. Monday night we spent in the China quarter, none of the others having ever seen a Chinaman at home. We went to the theatre, and a gambling-house, took tea with a China merchant, Sing Man, and finished the night at 2 a.m. in a European gambling-house, but did not gamble ourselves.

To-morrow we shall start from here at 4.0 in the afternoon, and ride forty-five miles back to Mariposa over the mountains—an awful journey, but it must be done at all hazards. We shall have sixteen hours' riding, on raw horses with Mexican saddles.

I will write again in a week or ten days and relate my adventures in the Yosemite valley.

We had a very hard week getting to the mountains, but we were fully repaid, and enjoyed the whole thing immensely. We started from San Francisco at 4 p.m. on Wednesday the 27th ult., and reached Stockton, about a hundred miles up the Sangoaquin river, at 4 a.m. next morning. We had written beforehand to engage a carriage, or wagon, as they call it, and a team of four horses, to take us as far as carriages can go, and by 5 a.m. on Thursday we were off for our first stage, Snelling, a town sixty-five miles from Stockton. This we reached at 7 p.m.

The road was very bad, deeply rutted, and in places a mere track—the country being a sandy plain, part of the Sacramento Basin lying between the Sierra Nevada and the coast ranges of California. The weather was intensely hot and dusty. The temperature is very uniform on the Pacific coast, and would consequently be delightful were it not for the dust. The rainfall is exceedingly small; the rain falls only during the winter, and then in showers only. The mornings are always hot, but at noon the sea-breeze blows in from the Golden Gate, spreading out fanwise until its influence is felt as far as the mountains. This is the great charm of the country. The plains are exceedingly fertile; great quantities of wheat and barley are grown, and there is a large export trade, extending even as far as England.

But California suffers from two great misfortunes; and these alone keep her from becoming the most flourishing State in the Union, and taking the lead in politics, commerce and society. One is that the land has all been bought up at high prices by speculators, so that immigration is at a standstill. The other is the high price of labour. The latter trouble can be cured by the free importation of Chinese labour; the

39

former is more difficult to deal with. The papers advocate legislation to prevent the speculators from buying up the land, but it is difficult to see how this can be done. In the unsurveyed districts a man may become a squatter; under the Homestead and Pre-emption Laws he can put in a claim, and when the land is surveyed and divided into sections and townships he can get his homestead free and pre-empt another 160 acres (or quarter-section) at the Government price of 1 dollar 25 cents per acre. The homestead also is 160 acres, so that he really gets 320 acres for about 200 dollars. But when all the land has been surveyed—and it is being surveyed as rapidly as possible—and after all claims have been put in, then the land comes into the market, and people buy it for speculation. California is the worst State in the Union for a poor immigrant, yet the land is the best and the most productive in the States, and the climate the healthiest by far. Lots of immigrants come, find the purchase of land beyond their means, and hire themselves out as labourers until they earn enough to return or else go in for mining, and in either case they go away abusing the country.

The Chinese will work wonders in California if they are allowed free access, but hitherto the lower classes, labourers, &c., have combined to exclude them or to place them under such disabilities that it is not worth their while to come. But they have defeated their own ends, and all the farmers, manufacturers and traders have combined to get Chinese labour at all costs, so that there will soon be 100,000 to 200,000 Chinamen hard at work. There is already one Chinaman for every twenty-five white men. The Chinese can live where a white man starves; they can do more work, man for man; and further, they are peaceful, contented, and highly civilized. I have always had a very high opinion of the Chinese people. I liked what I saw of them in their own country, and I like even more what I have seen of them in America.

I am afraid I am given to writing, in my letters, of subjects which interest me and possibly no one else; but in future I shall confine myself to a strict narrative of my travels, and avoid essays upon American politics.—At Snelling, which is a little agricultural town half-way to the mountains, we met a lot of miners who had found a wonderful fossil animal which they were taking to San Francisco, paying their way by charging fifty cents for a view of it. The landlord of the inn described it to me as the most wonderful thing ever found, with horns six feet long and three in circumference, inverted over its back. I told him that I was a geologist, so I was taken to examine it. I saw at once that it was the upper jaw and tusks of a mastodon, and I endeavoured to persuade the miners that the horns were tusks, and that the jaw was the upper and not the lower jaw. They would not be convinced but luckily I remembered that I had a geological textbook with me which contained a picture of a mastodon's head. I showed them this, and made them turn the skull over and compare it with the picture, when they were satisfied that I was right, and I at once became a great man in their eyes. Beach, Cheetham and Garlies took the miners' view for a time, but I think it was only to chaff me. They believed in me ever afterwards on geological questions. With this fossil were found several flint arrow-heads, proving that man was contemporary with the mastodon. This, however, was already known.

We left Snelling at 4 a.m. next morning, for Mariposa— thirty miles distant—which we reached at 12 p.m., after which we rested. We inspected the school, a small but very creditable establishment, and also went down into a quartz mine, the first real mine I ever inspected. We were rewarded by seeing a few specks of gold. The machine for crushing the quartz and catching the gold was very interesting. We left Mariposa next morning at 4 a.m., and made for Clark's Ranch, riding thirty miles through the mountains to a little wooden inn. We had a hot dusty ride, and at first found some difficulty in sitting on the hard, high-peaked Mexican saddles. Once we were accustomed to them we got on swimmingly. We had some dinner, and then rode on seven miles further to see the big trees which have caused so much excitement lately. They grow only here and there in the lower ranges of the Sierra, and are the largest trees in the world. They are about 300 in the grove which we saw, but they are interspersed over an area of perhaps a square mile of forest. The tallest is 325 feet in height, and the girth of one which we measured about 5 feet from the ground was 87 feet. The bark is about six inches thick. They were discovered only ten years ago, but are well known in England as the *Wellingtonia gigantea*. I have several cones full of seed picked up under the Diamond Group, which I hope will be perpetuated at Tibberton.[1]

We were awfully tired that night, and slept soundly till 3.30 a.m., when our inexorable guide made us get up and start for the Yosemite—another thirty miles' ride over a bad mountainous road. We carried our luggage with us—mine consisting of a great-coat, a sponge, and a toothbrush—*voilà tout*.

We reached the Yosemite valley at night, after riding thirteen hours, and were charmed with the first glimpse of the valley which we got before descending. The valley is Y-shaped, and is about a mile wide, with a river running down the middle. All around are lofty granite peaks and domes, and the walls of the valley are sheer precipices of

[1] The seeds were planted at his father's home in England, Tibberton, Gloucestershire, and grew into large trees. I cut one down in 1932.—M. P. P.

3,000 to 5,000 feet in height, with no ledge or terrace of rock to break the fall.

The valley is a geological puzzle, but it is supposed to be caused by a sudden subsidence, and I am satisfied that this is the case, as I observed that the granite had a slaty kind of cleavage which would permit of subsidence, assuming a hollow space beneath. As the valley is in the midst of the volcanic region of the mountains this can easily be accounted for.

The Yosemite valley was discovered only ten years ago, by a party of men hunting for stolen cattle. It was known that the Indians had some unknown fastness in the mountains to which they retreated when pursued, and these cattle-men were the first to stumble upon it during one of their expeditions.

They encamped in the valley, where they were set upon by the Indians and two of their number were killed. A war ensued, and all the Indians were killed with the exception of one or two, who still survive. The valley and the groves of the Big Trees were made over by the United States to the State of California for the perpetual recreation and resort of the inhabitants of the State, and can never be settled upon. The valley is 4,500 feet above sea-level, and the North Dome 6,700 feet higher still. Another mountain—the Clouds' Rest—is nearly 7,000 feet above the valley and 11,000 feet above sea-level.

We spent the whole of Monday in the valley, and as the weather was perfect, although so late in the season, we enjoyed ourselves immensely.—I forgot to mention an amusing hunt we had the previous day, while on our journey to the Yosemite. In a glade of the pine-forest, about half-way to the valley, our guide suddenly stopped, came stealthily back to us, and asked if anyone had a pistol. We none of us had, and were consequently somewhat alarmed, expecting either Indians or road-agents—i.e., highway robbers. The guide's excitement, however, was caused only by the sight of two nice lambs, quietly feeding and utterly unconscious of the sensation which their presence had aroused.

All kinds of cattle, horses and sheep that are turned out in the mountains during the summer are brought in about the end of October. Of course, numbers of them get lost, and the rule is recognized that after the animals have been collected and driven in, those that have strayed, except in the case of horses, are fair game for anyone who can catch them. As we did not expect to get any meat in the valley, the sight of these two lambs had much the same effect upon us as the manna in the wilderness upon the Israelites, except that the manna could not run away and the lambs could. We held a council of war and decided to pursue them—that is, the guide, Garlies and I did. Beach and Cheetham thought it wrong, though they thought it right to eat the lamb when captured. Perhaps they were only lazy. We three then surrounded the lambs, and charged down upon them, and after a vigorous pursuit, riding in the most reckless manner, jumping over trees, crashing through bushes and so on, one lamb, which was suffering either from heart-disease or weak lungs, was too done up to run farther, and our guide threw himself out of the saddle and on to the quarry and secured it. I got out my big knife and cut its throat, and so it became mutton. We dined off it that night, and finished it next day.

We left the valley at 3.30 a.m. on Tuesday morning, after getting Beach and Cheetham up with great difficulty. We had a cold ride until sunrise, got to Clark's Ranch at midday, dined, and rode on to Mariposa, getting in at 8.0 p.m., having ridden fifteen hours over forty-eight miles of mountain road. Next morning we were on our way to Stockton again, and did about sixty miles in our wagon, which had waited for us at Mariposa. We slept in a little wayside ranch, four in one room, and started again at 5 a.m. on the Thursday morning, doing the remaining thirty miles into Stockton in time to catch the train eastwards. Here Beach and Cheetham concluded to remain and rest after their unwonted labours, and dawdle about California. Garlies and I went on for Utah, reached Uintah Station on the Salt Lake at noon on Saturday, and took the stage for the forty miles to Salt Lake City, which we reached about 5.0 p.m.

We went that night to the theatre, and were much pleased and surprised by the Mormon acting. With the Mormons the theatre is a great institution. Brigham Young encourages it, and as far as he can makes it a school for the guidance of his flock. The theatre is very well-arranged and the scenery first-rate. Brigham Young has a sort of armchair as his special seat in the pit, or else one of the two private boxes, the other being retained for the use of the performers. He was not at the theatre that night, but a communicative Gentile who sat next to me pointed out several of his wives and children. I especially noticed three, called Net, Punk and Tabby, quite young and rather good-looking, but there was something about them which struck me especially. Punk and Tabby were very well dressed and piquant-looking. I should say they were lively, flirtatious girls. Net was more staid and pensive-looking. A very pretty girl indeed, dressed in quiet but full New York fashion, was Miss Stenhouse, daughter of a great Mormon light, the editor of the *Salt Lake Telegraph*. The Mormons all sit in the pit, 2nd circle and gallery. Gentiles sit only in the dress circle. They played *Griffith Gaunt*, and some of the characters were really first-class. A man named Majuts, an Englishman, played the gamekeeper capitally, and his broad Cumberland dialect was perfect. The fair scene was inimitable, and for spectators they brought up a lot of boys and girls out of the theatre, dressed in their ordinary clothes, just as they would be at a fair. And this made the scene as natural as reality. Generally at a theatre the *corps de ballet* is brought in, dressed up in fantastic peasant costume, to represent a crowd. Here we had a real crowd, not acting, but really enjoying the sights of the fair. One of Young's daughters took the part of "Alice," but she was not successful.

On Sunday we went to the Tabernacle in the morning, and heard two of the Apostles preach. They have no set service; exhortation is the main business of the meeting. George Teesdale preached for about an hour, a sensible, practical address, and George Cannon preached a short, fanatical sermon. In the afternoon we heard W. J. Smith, nephew to the founder of their religion, and a celebrated Mormon missionary and apostle, Wilford Woodruffe Smith, who was extremely dogmatical and fanatical. The other was like Teesdale, sensible and practical. The language of all the preachers was good and eloquent, but "homespun," as they say. There were two thousand persons present in the Tabernacle in the afternoon. I noticed the features of the congregation carefully, and I saw the same story told on each face. Restless, morbid excitement, coupled with a certain amount of intellect, just enough to make them throw off Calvinism and cling, as if in despair, to the supernatural to the extent of believing that such a man as Joseph Smith or Brigham Young could really be the instrument of revelation between God and Man. This I noticed among the better class, which was mainly Scottish and American in origin. The lower class was composed of stupid, stolid English, Germans and Swedes. The Englishmen and Germans were probably enticed by promises of land flowing with milk and honey, and as many wives as they could support. The idea of being gathered into the Valley of the Mountains, while the wrath of God swept over the face of the earth, passing

46

them over and leaving them to form the Kingdom of Christ for a thousand years, had little to do with their case. Mormonism is a great question for America, and I fear they will cut the Gordian Knot by persecuting them and driving them out. I have no sympathy whatever with the Mormons, but they have done wonders, and after all, polygamy has had no ill effect as yet. It is a step backward towards the civilization of the past. It does well enough in a little secluded territory out of reach of the world's influences, but would never suit modern civilization. Why not let it wear away, as it must do, now that Utah has become a great national highway? It has worked well enough hitherto, and the innumerable children of Utah are all wanted to develop the resources of the country.

The Americans, however, are bent on getting rid of the scandal, as they call it, and I am very sorry to think that such intolerance exists. They are busy through the Press misrepresenting the Mormons in every way, and by working upon the minds of the New England zealots they are preparing for a crusade, perhaps as early as next year.

We were very civilly received by Brigham Young, who seemed well acquainted with English politics. He was a shrewd, homely-looking man, giving one the idea of a self-made English merchant of the middle class. He told us he thought it a great thing that men in England should go into politics so young, but that they ought to listen for at least a year before they begin to speak.

I must now draw this letter to a close, as I am nearly exhausted by my efforts. We left Salt Lake on Tuesday and reached St. Louis yesterday (Friday) night. We gave up our Laramie trip; we stayed only a few hours there, and came on by the next train. St. Louis is a fine city, probably the finest in the West. The weather is bitterly cold, with snow thick on the ground. We hope to be in New Orleans by this day week.

I have had a very good time here, and I think have gathered a good deal of information on many important points. I am not the least shaken in my democratic opinions, but only strengthened, though I am at present rather disposed to be shaken in my faith in Free Trade as regards the interest of America. For heaven's sake don't tell anyone, and on no account Tom Potter,[1] for I have not yet made up my mind, and have no doubt that I shall return to my ancient faith. But I am by no means sure that the Republicans are not right as regards their own interest, and that America is not large enough, and her resources varied enough, to make it worth her while to constitute herself a gigantic Zollverein, depending entirely upon herself. I have not yet talked to the ironmasters and manufacturers of Pa. and New England, and there I shall probably be converted to Free Trade for America by those who advocate the Tariff. As yet the farmers and cotton-growers, whose interest plainly lies in Free Trade, and who advocate it, have rather shaken my belief: I hope, however, that the effect is only temporary.

I am confirmed in my opinions of the education question, and am delighted with the way in which the system works here. I believe the secret is in taxing the people. It dignifies the object for which they are taxed, because they see that it is important enough for the State to deal with it, and being taxed they think they may as well have their tax's worth: so they send their children to school. There is a stratum at the very bottom of society which legislation can never get at. Voluntary effort and charity can deal with it, and in America charitable institutions of this kind do an immense amount of good.

[1] A prominent Free Trader in England at this time.—M. P. P.

48

I like the Americans exceedingly, especially the Western men. These are a fine energetic race, the pith of New England, the stem of the Anglo-Saxon. I think they must have some connection with Flanders, for they swear dreadfully; but this is their only fault. I have as yet but little experience of the South, though I am now on the borders, where Southern sympathies are strong. Tomorrow we go to Louisville; we shall spend Monday at the Kentucky Caves, and then go to Memphis for a day. From Memphis we go to New Orleans, where I hope to be on Sunday next. I must miss Savannah, Charleston, &c. It is very vexatious, but the railway communications are very bad, and I cannot waste the time, as I *must* have a fortnight or ten days in Boston and New England generally. I shall go direct to Washington from New Orleans, do Richmond from there, and then go to Philadelphia for a day.

We arrived here on Saturday morning, after a week's hard travelling over a great deal of country.

There is a sameness about nearly all American cities which takes away from the interest in visiting them. They are all built on the same plan, and the streets generally have the same names.

The Kentucky Caves were very interesting. We took only the short route of about five miles, but the passages, they say, extend for about 200 miles. All the channels have been washed out at some remote period by the Green River, beds of gravel, silt and clay marking the action of the currents. The process is a chemical one, so the caves are not so wonderful as the cañons of the Rocky Mountains, where the channels have been cut, to a depth of 5,000 feet, in solid rock, solely by the action of the water.

Memphis is an interesting place enough. A great deal of cotton is shipped from there. We saw the process of cleaning and pressing the cotton by machinery, and there seemed to be a great deal of business going on. Jackson was crammed, as a State Fair was being held, and we could get no accommodation at the hotels. We just lay down on the floor of the bar-room. The New Orleans train left at 12.50 a.m., and as no sleeping-cars were on the train we had to pass the night without sleep in the smoking-car, with lots of negroes about us. These, as emancipation has not deodorized them, are not pleasant travelling-companions. When we reached New Orleans we had been sixty hours without taking off our clothes, or even our boots, or washing.

This is a splendid city, the finest I have yet seen. It has a foreign look, but half the city is still French, and the French language is still spoken here. The streets are wide and well paved, and the houses well built. There is a pleasing variety in the façades of all the houses, no one being like another; old and new are mixed up together, which relieves the eye from the monotony of a street where all the houses are alike. This is the great failing of American cities. I have several friends here, and we are almost overwhelmed with hospitality. I have made the acquaintance of numbers of people, and I am bound to say that Southerners, so far as I can see, still sustain their reputation for culture and polish above all other Americans. The girls are very handsome, a plain-looking girl being quite the exception. But I should say they were regular tigers when roused. It is amusing to hear them talk of the war. The feeling against the Yankees is *intense*, and I must admit the Yankees give them good cause for hatred. The South has been shamefully plundered, and, as a thorough-paced Republican, I am heart-broken by the gigantic system of corruption which prevails everywhere from high to low. Office is only a means of making a fortune. Every vote in the Legislature is for sale, white or black, and as far as I can see the same thing prevails everywhere, except in California, where politics is tolerably incorrupt, and, as I am told, in New England. The military Governors of the reconstructed Southern States have plundered them in the most shameful manner, if one can believe the statements one hears in New Orleans. Butler seized every article of value he could find in this city, even to silver forks and spoons, and I have heard many stories of the ruses which the people adopted to save their plate from Butler's rapacious hand.

The negroes here are very different animals from their Northern brothers. They are a low, uneducated, brutal set, but little removed from barbarism. Of course, all this is the result of slavery, and, as I told a Southern friend yesterday, it is a disgrace to the Southern people for having clung to slavery and not to the North for giving the negroes political rights.

I am quite in favour of negro suffrage, for I believe the upper class could still control the negroes and lead them if they would. But they won't. They stand aloof with their arms folded, and say, "Look what your policy has brought us to—negro justices and negro members: we can't associate with them, even for the good of the country." And so they are governed by them and the unscrupulous radicals in authority; the Governors, the Secretary of State, &c., leading the negro legislators by their noses. A thousand dollars buys a judgeship, because whomsoever the Governor nominates the negroes elect. And yet the suffering people of the South so dislike the negro coming between them and their nobility that they won't throw their influence into the scale and oppose the prevailing corruption. Election to office in this State is a farce, for the Governor takes everything into his own hands, although the State is reconstructed.

I arrived here on Saturday night, after a week's hard travelling through Mississippi, Alabama, Georgia and Virginia, which almost tired me out.

I left New Orleans by myself, Garlies having gone into Georgia to see some friends there. We got only as far as Canton, about 150 miles, when we came to a stop, owing to some accident to the engine, and there we had to stay from 4 a.m. to 8 p.m. I spent the day in going over a cotton plantation, so I suppose I may consider that I lost nothing by the delay. That night we went on, and got a sleeping-car, but were turned out at 3.30 a.m., although we had been promised that the sleeping-car should go through to Chattanooga.

It was very cold and disagreeable, but we had to turn out, and I began to wish myself at home again. On reaching Chattanooga we missed the connection with the Knoxville train, and had to stay there till the following morning. This did not disconcert me much, as I wanted to see the place. It is prettily situated in a corner of the mountains between Missionary Ridge and Look-out Mountain, on the Tennessee River. A great deal of fighting took place during the war near Chattanooga, and Grant gained his most decisive victory over the Confederates at Look-out Mountain. A short time before this the Federals were beaten at Chickamanga, and retreated into Chattanooga, which was then invested by the Confederates and relieved by Grant and Sherman.

Next day we proceeded along the Tennessee valley, and between the Cumberland and Alleghany Mountains, to Knoxville, where there was a delay. There I saw the entrenchments of the Federals, and the battlefield of Knoxville, where the Confederates were beaten by Rosencranz. On

53

Friday night we arrived at Bristol, the border town of Virginia and Tennessee, half the town lying in either State. Next morning at daylight we were running through a gap in the Alleghanies, down the valley of the James River, to Lynchberg, where we breakfasted. We passed during the day the battlefields of the Wilderness, Manasses, Culpeper and Bull Run, though the country does not by any means present the appearance of having been ravaged as we learn it to have been. I got into Washington by dark, but as I have not been out yet I can tell you nothing about it.

I enjoyed my stay in New Orleans immensely. We were most hospitably treated, and made the acquaintance of lots of people. The Southern girls are certainly exceedingly handsome, and their society is quite different from that of the North. They have all spent some years in Europe, especially in France, and their manners are quite French, except that they have no reserve whatever, and talk quite freely and easily, without expecting to be talked to and complimented as the French girls do. We went twice to the Opera and once to a dinner-party, but they don't do much in the latter line since the war.

General Butler stole all their plate and all their wines, and there was an immense amount of genteel poverty amongst them, which they don't like to confess. You never see them driving out, and they hardly ever give dinner-parties. Their chief object, in our case, was to convince us that they were the cultivated and aristocratic portion of American society, and no doubt they are, but I don't think any the better of them for that. They are aristocrats at heart: they hate the Liberal North, and still pretend that the negro was born to be a slave.

I left Washington on Wednesday night, after seeing the opening of Congress, got to Philadelphia at 2 a.m. on Thursday and went on to New York by the midday train.

I am going out to dinner tonight, at the house of one of the old Dutch families, the Knickerbockers, as they are called. The old Dutch families consider that they stand at the head of New York Society; this opinion is not shared by others. They are the most aristocratic, and I believe the most exclusive set, and they live among themselves in great style. They look down upon the "shoddy" aristocracy, as indeed they may well do, but I like best the set to which my friend Duncan and the Browns belong; which has no particular name, but which is more English than the others. I enjoyed myself immensely at the Duncans' last night, and Mrs. Duncan is the most charming woman. Yet she was only one of half a dozen equally charming. I must say I think that any young Englishmen who want to marry (*I* don't mean to, but this is for those that do), would do wisely to come to America for their wives. They can find beauty, money and talent, without the trouble of looking for them, and I shall certainly advise my friends to patronize the American matrimonial market, and so infuse a little fresh blood into our sluggish old country. Still, my sluggish old country has a good many charms for me, and I am very anxious to get back again. Politics and local matters, if nothing else, would be inducement enough to make me leave on the 11th.

December 10, 1869.

I left New York on Sunday for New London in Connecticut, to stay with my friend Stuart. He lives in a wild place overlooking the Atlantic, but has a very comfortable house, and English servants. He enabled me to get a good idea of New England life, and indeed I have got more genuine, reliable information during the last fortnight, respecting many of the most important political questions, than during all the rest of the trip.

Stuart drove me round the country, and took me to see the Roman Catholic priest, who enlightened me on the Fenian question, and a more important question still—that of the Irish-American influence which is threatening this country with such disaster; in fact, he showed me all that was to be seen.

I arrived at Boston on Monday night, and next morning I started for Tewkesbury in Massachussetts.[1] I have forgotten to say that we had a most terrible snowstorm, which began on Monday afternoon and continued until Tuesday night. The weather has been very cold for some days, and about six inches of frozen snow covered the ground. The rivers were freezing up, and all navigation was stopped up country. Then came the twenty-four hours' snow, and at 10 a.m. on Sunday morning, in the thick of the storm, I started for Tewkesbury. I could only get within four miles of it, by taking the train to Billericay, where I found half a dozen houses, a small wooden station, and one solitary man, the station-master. He gave me the pleasant information that Tewkesbury was four miles off, and that the only way to get

[1] My father was Member of Parliament for Tewkesbury in England.—M. P. P.

56

there was to walk. I tried this for 100 yards, but as the snow had drifted, and was still falling and drifting, and a keen North-eastern wind was blowing, I soon saw that I should be in an even worse mess than I was when I crossed the Terai Pass in the Himalayas. However, a small boy saw me returning, and on ascertaining that I wanted to go to Tewkesbury, he said he could get a horse and sleigh and drive me. I closed with this; he went and got a sleigh, and we started. Before we had gone a mile the wind was so keen and the cold so intense that the boy wanted to turn back, saying that his hands were so cold that he was afraid they were frostbitten. I was nearly frozen myself, and would have given worlds to have turned back, but I was on my mettle, so I determined to persevere, and, if necessary, drive myself. We reached the place at last, and I then found out the Town Clerk, who informed me that the nine selectmen were all away. The Chairman came only once a week, being engaged all the rest of the time as a County Commissioner, and the other two members of the Board resided, one in Boston, and the other two miles away.

I gave the Town Clerk my documents and views of our Tewkesbury, and requested him to lay them before the Board at the next meeting, and to communicate with me in England. The snow was so deep that I could not get much idea of the place, but it is a mere village of 1,000 inhabitants.

Next day I received an almost royal reception in Gloucester. Here is the invitation issued to all the officials and notables of the town and neighbourhood: "Dear Sir, The Selectmen of Gloucester would be pleased to have your Company at the reception of the Hon. W. E. Price, a Citizen of the City of Gloucester and Member of Parliament for Tewkesbury, England, to be given at the Pavilion Wednesday December 8th at 1.30 p.m. Dinner at 2.0 p.m." I was met at the train at nine o'clock, and proceeded to breakfast with the Chairman of the Selectmen; then a grand sleigh with two horses appeared, and I was taken round the town, and to all the places of interest in the neighbourhood. I then visited the schools, the Churches, and the Town Hall, and made a speech at the High School to an audience of about fifty young ladies and as many boys.

At the Reception I held a sort of *levée*, and about sixty people were introduced to me. Then came the Dinner, which was very good, except that we had only water to drink. After dinner the Mayor's letter was opened and read, and the President read a long address of his own, which I presume will be printed as a speech. He concluded by proposing the Queen. He then gave "the City of Gloucester," to which I responded in a long speech, which luckily I had to a certain extent prepared. Several other toasts followed, and then the health of "Our Distinguished Visitor" was given, and in it reference was made to the *Alabama* question and the unfriendly feeling of England during the war. This gave me an opportunity, and I made a smart speech, I can assure you. I gave the "England of the aristocracy" a rap over the knuckles. But I cannot go into further details now. Perhaps I may write again on board. I should only add that in the grace before meat "Our Distinguished Visitor" was prayed for, &c., &c., in a way that would have made me blush, if it hadn't made me laugh. The grace took five minutes, and the toasts were all drunk in bumpers of water. Gloucester (Mass.) is teetotal, as indeed nearly all New England is.

A few days after this Captain Price sailed for England.

Part Two

1878

MAJOR AND MRS. PRICE'S
AMERICAN TOUR

Extract from Letter of Major Price

PALMER HOUSE, CHICAGO.
Thursday, August 15, 1878.

. . . We arrived here this evening after travelling through from Montreal—thirty-four hours without a break. I propose to stay here tomorrow, to rest, make arrangements for roughing it in the Rocky Mountains, and rearrange our baggage. We shall leave for Denver, Colorado *via* Kansas City. . . . The Grand Trunk Railway is immensely improved, but I don't know whether Hickson's management has anything to do with it. It is well laid, well ballasted, and runs as smoothly as the best English line, and it has drawing-room cars and sleeping-cars in abundance. An American told me that he thought it was now the best managed line on the continent. I see great changes and great improvements, both in Canada and America. Eight years is a long time in these days of progress.

Chicago was nearly all burnt down three years ago, but the process seems to have improved it. It was thought that in consequence of the destruction of property by the fire Chicago would lose a great deal of its commercial importance in favour of St. Louis and Cincinnati. This has not been the case, however; on the contrary, its trade has increased enormously, in consequence of the development of the cattle trade with England. We passed a number of freight trains loaded with cattle, sheep and pigs, all going over the Grand Trunk to Quebec for shipment to England. Before long we shall draw most of our meat supplies from the Western prairies, and our English farmers must content themselves with wheat at four shillings and threepence a bushel!

Just now Canadian and American politics are very much

61

concerned with the Free Trade question. In Canada the approaching elections are to be fought on that platform, and the fate of the present Liberal Ministry depends on the result. They are in favour of a small tariff, 17½ per cent; the Conservatives want 25 per cent to 30 per cent, avowedly to exclude English manufactures. How many English farmers, if they could only get someone to advocate their views, would like the Corn Laws re-introduced and foreign cattle excluded! It astonishes me that when all the Colonies are Protectionist, the Mother Country remains true to Free Trade, even in her greatest depression.

Extract from a letter from Mrs. W. E. Price

PALMER HOUSE, CHICAGO.
August 16, 1878.

. . . We arrived here yesterday at 8 p.m., after two days' and a night's journey from Montreal. The railway travelling seems to me very easy, such pains is taken to make people comfortable, and there is a man to look after the passengers in each carriage, who always seems to have plenty to do. We had a little room in the carriage to ourselves, and at night regular beds are made, with sheets, &c. I was as comfortable as possible. We passed the frontier into the States in the morning, where they examined the luggage. The check system they have for the luggage is very convenient; they give you a metal number for each box, and you have no trouble at all in looking after it as in England. The train stops about twenty minutes for breakfast, dinner and tea, otherwise they stop a very short time at places, and sometimes go very quickly. The country through which we passed was very flat and well cultivated, richer and with

62

better fences than about Quebec and east of that town. The scenery was more English than I expected. There were potatoes and cabbage, Indian corn and tobacco, and always, in the large gardens, sunflowers. It is greener than usual for the time of year. . . . I like the Pullman cars very much. There is more room in them than in an ordinary carriage, and you can wash your hands in them as often as you please. The conductor will dust you with a feather brush, and you are offered newspapers, apples, and pears, and almost everything you can think of, by men who carry them through the train. After lunch Willie smokes on one of the platforms, and extracts information from some American who talks through his nose. At a junction called Detroit we went over part of a great railway carriage manufactory, where over 1,000 workmen were employed. Sometimes they make fifteen carriages a day. We saw the mould where the metal was poured on the moulded sand, and a wonderful knife which cut thick bars of iron most easily, made of Bessemer steel. The carriage-wheels are forced on to the axles by enormous pressure. We saw a great deal in a short time while we waited for the train. Mr. Pullman has sent Willie a general order that we are to be well looked after on the railways. I have just been with Willie to his office here; he is away in New York. We also went to the bank for money. In the room where we waited telegrams on slips of paper came in every minute, and the heads of the place kept coming to look at them, asking through their noses—"How's gold?" These telegrams told them the price of gold in all parts of Europe. . . .

Extract from a Letter from Major Price

AMERICAN HOUSE,
(J. U. Marlow, Proprietor),
DENVER, COLORADO.
Wednesday, August 20, 1878.

We reached here last night, and leave again to-morrow
morning for Colorado Springs, Manitou, and Este's Park in
the Rocky Mountains. We went the first thing this morning
to the First National Bank, to draw money and ask for letters.

The heat is terrific, and in Chicago very relaxing and
disagreeable. The town is low, and damp, below the level
of Lake Michigan in fact, and the sun is almost tropical.

We left Chicago at 10.30 Saturday, travelled through to
Omaha—500 miles—which we did in twenty-four hours,
changed at Omaha on Sunday, left about 12.30, and reached
Denver *via* Cheyenne at 9 o'clock last night, Monday.

The change which has come over America in eight years
is enormous, and I cannot tell you how impressed I am with
the wealth, strength, and latent power of the great Republic.
In another fifty years it will be the greatest power on earth.
There has been nothing like it in the history of the world.
It runs from the tropics nearly to the Arctic Circle; it
possesses millions and millions of acres of a fertility superior
to the Nile Valley, it can produce wheat and meat to feed the
world, and all the metals and minerals that are used in every
department of industry. For 500 miles from Chicago to
Omaha we saw nothing but large farms and busy cities,
with millions of acres of Indian corn and wheat on either
side of the line, as far as the eye could reach.

The old snake fences have disappeared. Neat hedgerows
have taken their place; round the homesteads are plantations
of trees, and labour, our great difficulty, is simply unneces-
sary. Very little manuring is done, so great is the fertility

64

of the land, and every variety of agricultural implement is to be found, even on the farm of the poorest squatter. All the corn grown anywhere near the railways is sold for export. Beyond the network of railways it is used to feed pigs and cattle and horses, which are shipped to England in immense quantities, either dead or alive. I predict that in a few years' time the export of horses to Europe will be enormous.

For a couple of hundred miles beyond Omaha the same condition of things exists. The higher you get the less Indian corn is grown, but agricultural operations shade off gradually from high cultivation to stock-breeding on an enormous scale, on prairies which twenty years ago supported nothing but buffalo, antelope and prairie dogs.

About 200 miles from Omaha we reached the limit of high cultivation, and these two hundred miles have been won since my last visit. After this the line passes through the boundless prairie until it reaches the foot of the Rocky Mountains, when it again passes through a belt of extreme fertility, the district where the Colorado wheat is grown. For ninety miles, from Cheyenne to Denver, running due south, we passed cornfields as red as sunset, the wheat just being cut, but of the deepest red, rich ears, and scanty straw. These settlements are from five to ten years old. Rain never falls there in the summer; it is burning hot, but as the elevation is 6,000 feet the nights are cool, and the neighbouring mountains yield a never-failing supply of water, which is brought over the fields in what they call *acequias*—the Spanish word for irrigation-channels.

How far south this goes I don't know, but I shall go down as near Santa Fé in New Mexico as I can. Colorado has just been admitted as a State, and it will before long be one of the most powerful States in the Union. It has coal, gold, silver, wheat of the very finest quality in the world, much used for biscuit-baking, and livestock to any amount; and the Colorado beetle is a delusion, at least as far as the reports which come to England are concerned. Occasional visits of grasshoppers are much more dreaded.

We were lucky enough at Omaha to fall in with General Sherman, Commander-in-Chief of the American Army, his A.D.C. and Military Secretary, General McCook, and a Major Turner, a retired officer, but a great friend of General Sherman's.

We soon became great friends, and they have been most attentive to us. We are with them now, and start to-morrow morning with them for Manitou.

Sherman is a fine fellow, the best soldier the States have produced, a shrewd, clever man of the world, but exceedingly refined and gentlemanly. Maggie is delighted with him.

They will give us letters which will be most useful. We shall be in San Francisco about 5th of September, and start on 10th for Portland, Oregon Territory, on the Columbia River three days by steamer, then by a small railway, lately built through Washington Territory, to Puget Sound, and thence by steamer to Victoria in Vancouver Island. I mean to see New Mexico and Arizona as well.

General Sherman is now on his way to Santa Fé, the chief town of New Mexico, and I have a most inordinate longing to go there. It was an early Mexican settlement, and most of the scenes of Mayne Reid's novels—the *Scalp Hunters* and others—were laid in that district. It is sub-tropical in temperature and flora, and inhabited chiefly by Mexicans and Indians. The fiercest Indians inhabited this district, and none but the hardiest trapper ever ventured there. During the last twenty years repeated expeditions of U.S. troops have brought the Indians to their senses by killing and deporting them, and the place is safe enough now. One may got robbed, but if one carries very little with one it doesn't matter. They don't kill people, or take them off and put them to ransom as they do in Greece and Sicily.

There is a great deal of mining there, and although the mining population is a shifting one, yet, taking the Mexicans into consideration, the population is large enough to entitle the Territory to become a State. Congress, however, very properly objects to make the change, as the Mexican element is not a very desirable one to introduce as a factor in American politics. The Denver and Rio Grande Railway runs southwards along the Rocky Mountains to a place called Fort Garland, about 120 miles from Santa Fé, and I should not wonder if we made the journey. Maggie is most anxious to go. On the Californian side I shall go down by a railway just open to Los Angeles, and on to Yuma City on the great Colorado River, which enters the Pacific at the junction of the State of California and the Territory of Arizona. I should like to get a trip up the river to the Colorado Cañon, but I am afraid this can't be done. I think if I carry out my programme and see Oregon and Washington Territories, and our Colony of British Columbia and Vancouver Island, and also penetrate New Mexico on the east, and Arizona on the west of the Rocky Mountains, I shall have shown Maggie a good deal of the out-of-the-way parts of the American continent. She is very well, except a little cold she has caught, but I think it is only a congestion from the sun in Chicago. Tomorrow we shall get up to 8,000 feet and the next day go up Pike's Peak—14,000 feet—which will soon put ailments of that kind right.

The heat is terrible here, I am dripping with perspiration, and it is falling in regular drops from the tip of my nose on to the blotting paper.

About a hundred Ute Indians are in Denver, with their squaws, papooses, and ponies. They have just returned from buffalo hunting on the Republican River, and are now trading.

Extract from a Letter from Mrs. W. E. Price

August 20, 1878.

. . . It was from Spanish Peaks in Colorado that we started with General Sherman to go to Santa Fé. We first met the General on the Pacific Railway as we were crossing the continent, and I well remember how the train was waiting at a small place called Boulder City, and how as I was sketching the town from the window of the car the General came up to me and asked to look at my sketch, saying that he knew something of the art. I expressed the wish that he would give me his opinion and help in the matter, and he then talked on for some time. He was one of the best-informed men I have ever met (Professor Huxley being another, though of a different stamp). Both these men had, I thought, a wonderful fascination about them. The General's knowledge of all sorts of things was wonderful. . . . From Denver we went to Manitou by train, a sort of watering-place. Sulphur, iron and soda springs come up separately, close to one another. It is a pretty place, in a valley, right in the Rocky Mountains. We found it hot—very hot at night, and unappetizing, but the food they gave us was certainly bad. We rode with a guide to the summit of Pike's Peak. We had to go in Indian file almost the whole way, first through a beautiful valley, full of enormous granite boulders and fir-trees. It was very steep, and generally the track was narrow. We once met some loaded donkeys, and their driver refusing to turn back for a short distance we had difficulty in passing. I thought our party would have to lie down while the donkeys walked over us like the celebrated goats! Though we had started at 7 a.m., the sun soon became very hot: sometimes I thought I could never reach the top, and then perhaps a small cloud would give me shade for a few minutes, or we would come to some trees. I had a capital pony and a comfortable saddle. We rode twenty miles. It was a rise of about 8,000 feet from Manitou. We stopped at a half-way house for about ten minutes, and then on again. The last part, going up, was quite bare, and extremely rough, with great stones everywhere. There was a sort of track, and heaps of stones to show the way in snow. Below the path was marked sometimes by the trees being blazed. When we reached the top lunch was our first idea, we were all so hungry. The guide said the food was "demoralized," for it had been squeezed together by knocking against the donkeys who would not turn back for us. However, I know I was very glad of the demoralized food, and did justice to it. Then I looked about to see if I could draw, which was rather absurd, considering we were 14,149 feet above the sea. The view over the plain was quite wonderful, but the rarity of the atmosphere made one feel faint and breathe twice as quickly as usual. The descent was the most tiring part of the trip, and we took twenty minutes' rest by a stream for the horses to eat some grass. We were away twelve hours exactly. . . . Next day we were to go a two days' expedition down south, to a place called Alamosa, a town which has sprung up entirely in the last two months. Of course, it is not a very elegant place. There was a large store where everything could be bought, from ladies' gloves to saddles, knives, glass, cart-grease, &c. The hotel was nice. It had been moved fifteen times, always going to the town where the railway ended for the time. It was a day's railway-journey to this place, over a fine pass, which is the second highest in America. We were with General Sherman's party, if one may so call it, for the General makes friends with everyone he travels with. There were some very bright, amusing American girls: we thought them great fun, but it takes a little time for me to get used to their difference from us. During supper at the "Wandering Hotel" General Sherman said that if Willie and I would like to join him and General McCook on the expedition they were then commencing (with reference to the Indians) as far as Santa Fé, there was an empty ambulance to spare in which we and a bag or two could travel. He said they would make it as comfortable for me as they could, but that we should have to camp out in the open some two nights or so. I could sleep in the ambulance, but of course it would be rough. . . . I said I would go. So we started at 9 a.m. (the American girls envying me very much). . . .

Extract from letter from Major Price

August 29, 1878.

. . . We left Manitou on Friday morning, took the train at Colorado Springs, and travelled till six o'clock at night over the Colorado plains, parallel with the Rocky Mountains. At a place called Cucharas the railway bifurcates, the Western branch crossing the Sangre de Cristo Range, the Eastern running down parallel with the main ridge, which here rises up in two conical peaks, called the Spanish Peaks, to a place called El Moxo, about fifty miles farther south. This is the terminus on the eastern side. We were bound westward. From Cucharas the line passes up a slow ascent to La Veta, and there the train is lightened, and an extra engine is added; it then crosses the Veta mountain, 11,500 feet high, over a pass 9,339 feet above sea-level, the highest railway pass in the world except one in Peru.

We took an hour and a half reaching the summit, winding round and round the mountain up a gredient of 1 in 25. On reaching the top, the train runs rapidly down into the San Luiz Park, a great table-land in the headwaters of the

Rio Grande del Norte, where a new "city" has just been laid out, called Alamosa, or the "Poplar City." In America, when they lay out a town or city, they select the site and plant poplars or cottonwood trees to mark the streets. In a year or two, when the trees begin to grow, the lots are taken up and houses built, and if the site is favourable, in a few years a great city springs up. When I was at Denver eight years ago it had not long been settled. Now it is a populous city of 20,000 inhabitants. In all probability Alamosa, in ten years' time, will also be a city of 20,000 inhabitants. At present it consists of about twenty wooden houses, a few tents, and a hotel that has "travelled" several hundred miles. Notwithstanding this, there is hardly an article of food or clothing, knick-nack or toy, that one could not purchase at one of the five or six stores established there.

General Sherman had ordered accommodation for our party, and I don't know how it was managed but they did contrive to house and feed the whole party of thirteen, and very well indeed too. General Sherman's train of ambulances, &c., had been sent to meet him there from Santa Fé, and he offered us one of the ambulances if we liked to accompany him thither. . . . We started on Saturday morning, the 24th, on a five days' march—it is 140 miles to Santa Fé.

Our journey the first day was about thirty miles over a perfectly flat sandy plain, very dusty, and covered with nothing but the sage-bush, a sort of wormwood growing in bushes. The two Generals went on first in an ambulance with four mules and a driver, Maggie and I next in ditto, and a covered wagon with six mules carrying provisions and tents, hay, &c. All the morning we walked or trotted gently along a track over a very wide plain. At 12 o'clock we reached a river, and drank, out of tin canteens, water yellow with mud. We ate biscuits and meat out of tins. Off again in a quarter of an hour, and now it was very hot, and the two

Generals in front stirred up clouds of dust, so we were obliged to keep at a respectful distance. Sometimes the front ambulance was quite obscured from view. We saw sand whirling up in long columns like waterspouts, and skeletons of horses and cattle lying about.

We halted at Conejes, a Mexican village built entirely of adobe or sunburnt bricks, and inhabited by half-breed Mexicans, the descendants of the old Spanish colonists and the Indians. The houses are very quaint, one storey high, with very thick walls and flat roofs, made of laying poles crosswise over the walls and covering them two feet thick with mud. A veranda projects from the house, built of poles, and roofed in the same manner.

We were put up at the house of the principal inhabitant of the district, a Major Head who had formerly served with General McCook. Head had married a Mexican half-breed, about the ugliest woman I ever saw. We were waited on by two young Navajo Indians, and if our meals had been at a reasonable hour I should have said we fared very well. As it was we had nothing from breakfast at seven o'clock until 5 p.m., two hours after arriving at Conejes, when they served us with what they call supper. This consisted of trout, mutton ribs grilled, eggs, ham, and coffee. From 6 p.m. till 6.0 the next morning we had nothing.

The pueblo or village of Conejes was very interesting, as the first Mexican village we were able to inspect. Of course, the inhabitants were all Roman Catholics, and at Conejes there was a Jesuit establishment or a nunnery. The chapel consists of an ordinary adobe house, one storey high, rectangular in shape, and two poles stuck up crosswise, with a bell hanging from the angle, formed the belfry. The faithful were invited to prayers by a man striking the clapper against the bell. We witnessed that evening one of the heaviest thunderstorms I have ever seen. It thunders, of course, every day in these parts, but a special storm was turned on that night for our benefit. It commenced about three in the afternoon, and by nightfall it closed in all round; and from 2 a.m. the lightning was incessant. Rain fell in torrents in the mountains, but spared us. Unfortunately, however, it washed away six miles of the railroad back to Denver, and our retreat is cut off. . . .

Extract from letter from Mrs. W. E. Price

August 26, 1878.

As we were travelling on Sunday the 25th there was the most alarming thunderstorm I ever was in. I never moved out of the ambulance all day, as I should have been wetted through by the downpour, and I was so restricted as to luggage that I had only the dress I was wearing with me. Our two hand-bags and some wraps were all we had. The lightning and thunder came at the same moment, and struck a tree close by. How we escaped I don't know. It was most unpleasant. No one was comfortable except the stolid mules. Willie got out at an encampment during the storm. There were only a few tents; no houses. In the evening we encamped at Las Piedras among pine-trees. The storm had ended. The men made a camp fire, pitched the General's tent, and picketed the mules. We had tea in a log hut, served by an Indian woman. She was the prettiest woman, except Lady Granville, that I have ever seen, and had the most refined manners. The bread she made was capital. She offered me her bed for the night, but I preferred to sleep in the ambulance, as I thought it would be cleaner. General Sherman insisted on my taking one of his pillows. I slept most comfortably in the ambulance. Willie slept in the other, and the two Generals in a tent. The mules were picketed near by, and at night a wolf came and howled, but I did not hear it.

Extract from a letter from Major Price (continued)

August 29, 1878.

...Our route lay over sandy plains till we descended through a forest of cedar bushes and dwarf pines to a lower plain or steppe, much broken up by granitic outcrop and covered by very creditable specimens of red pine. Here we came into the very centre of another thunderstorm which scared both us and our mules, as three or four flashes of lightning fell close to us. We closed up our ambulance wagons and ate our lunch of biscuit and water, and when the storm had passed we went on to our bivouac for the night at Las Piedras. Here we pitched our tent, lit a fire in spite of the rain, and had a very pleasant evening round the camp fire, with the two Generals recounting their various military adventures. I learnt a good deal from General Sherman, who is the one really good and scientific general in the U.S. Army.

Extract from Letter from Mrs. W. E. Price

SANTA FÉ.
August 29, 1878.

Next day we reached Ojo Caliente or "Burning Eye" or "Spring." This is a hot sulphur spring. Here we spent a bad night, as the place simply swarmed with creatures. We ought to have slept in our clothes, as the Generals did. On again next morning. The scenery was now different from anything we had seen before—soil red and sandy, rivers muddy, and air so clear that distant bushes and objects appeared quite near. That evening we reached San Juan, a most curious place, consisting of one store, kept by a German, a Roman Catholic church with a Frenchman as Curé, and the rest of the population Pueblo Indians, the descendants of the old

74

Mexicans or Aztecs. The entrance to the houses is from the roof, which is reached by a ladder and from the roof another ladder leads down into the house. I could hardly climb the ladders, the rungs were so far apart. We went to the house of the Chief, and were invited to sit on low seats close to the wall. The Chief talked bad Spanish and was very polite. His squaw brought a plate of apples and offered us one each, while two grinning Indian girls looked at us from the corner. They are most picturesque people, especially the women, in their long, dull green and red shawls, carrying large black jars on their heads. The style of architecture in these villages dates back to the old days when they were at war with the white man and their Northern fellow-Indians, the Comanches Apaches and Utes. These Pueblo Indians are the "tame Indians," cultivating the soil and managing their own affairs with a certain amount of success.

On approaching Santa Fé, the capital of New Mexico, an escort of twelve officers came out to meet the Generals. They were dressed in various uniforms, and looked very different from our English soldiers. Though it was raining hard the people all seemed to be looking out for General Sherman, and salutes were fired as he passed. We are now staying here as the guests of Major and Mrs. Whitehead, and are very comfortable after our rather rough travelling. The wife and daughter and little girl are the ladies of the party. With one servant-girl they do all the cooking and household work. Mrs. W. is now making herself a dress for a ball which is to be given to-night in honour of General Sherman. The latter has just given me a very good photograph of himself. We were very hungry on arriving here, and a meal chiefly of melon, which I don't like, we found barely satisfying. But they are most kind to us, and have given us their own room. At the head of the bed I found a loaded pistol, necessary in these parts. I am rather dreading the stage journey back in a "buckboard"; they say it is very rough. At one hill we are advised to get out and walk. It is a two days' and one night's journey.

Extract from Letter from Major Price

DENVER.
September 3, 1878.

We got back to Manitou last night, after sixty hours' incessant travelling, forty-eight hours of it on a "buckboard," over mountains and through rivers, and the rest by railway, and I was so done up that I was quite unable to write. I am all right this morning, and so is Maggie, but the expedition to Santa Fé was a strenuous one.

In the first place, it took ten days, and as I must leave San Francisco for Portland on September 10th, I was pressed for time. Then only four people can leave Santa Fé daily, the "buckboard" accommodating only that number, so it was three days before we could get places. I cannot adequately describe the horrors of travelling by "buckboard." It is a vehicle constructed for the roughest usage; it has no springs, and is merely a framework of open boards resting on four wheels, sometimes with an awning stretched over the top. It can go over mountains, almost down precipices, and certainly down and up deep gulleys at an angle of 80°, and the jolting, shaking, twisting and wriggling is indescribable. We spent two days and two nights in this conveyance, halting only twice a day for half an hour, for food.

However, we are quite recovered after a night's rest, and our journey to Santa Fé is a memory of the past. In a year or two the railway will be open, and then the romance of the visit will be destroyed.

The town itself is a very old one, established about

1650 by the Mexicans, who were attracted by reports of gold in the district. They suffered severely at the hands of the Indians, but eventually incorporated the country with Mexico, and it was taken from them, together with Texas, Colorado, Arizona and California, only after the Mexican War. It is now a United States Territory, and it might be a State, but for the dislike of the Americans to admit the Mexican-Indian population to State privileges. Spanish is the universal language of the country and the law-courts, and very few of the people speak English.

I have been talking Spanish freely during the trip, and indeed German and French too, for the storekeepers are mostly Germans, and the Roman Catholic priests French.

The town consists of an aggregation of adobe houses, surrounding a rank, weed-grown Plaza; the old Spanish Government House, built of adobe, one storey high, is now the residence and offices of the United States Governor and the State officials. There are some infantry and cavalry here, under the command of a General, but the men are nearly all out on escort duty, or on service in the different forts scattered over Arizona and New Mexico.

When General Sherman left with his escort of ten men, there remained *nine officers*, three sergeants, and *one* negro trooper.

Major Whitehead, who put us up, was very hospitable, but we were very uncomfortable notwithstanding. The habits of certain Americans are very different from ours.

They breakfast at 8.0, have no lunch, dine at 3.0 to 5.0, and spend long evenings in helping each other to do nothing.

Then we could get not a drop of wine or beer or whisky. On the second day, however, I was offered one glass of beer. The irregularity of our meals rather upset my liver, living as we were not in the desert, but in a well-built, well-appointed house.

77

We had no change of clothes, and Maggie had linen only for two days, yet we had to receive endless visits from the officials and officers of the district, and to return them, and we actually went to a ball given in honour of General Sherman, I in a shooting-jacket and thick shoes, and Maggie in her one very dirty dress, and we were obliged to dance several dances. It was the oddest ball I ever attended, but there were about a hundred people present, including lots of ladies, officers' wives and daughters, all very oddly dressed.

New Mexico, I think, may have a great future. Where water is attainable the soil is most fertile. The climate is sub-tropical, and produces every variety of magnificent fruit. It has coal, iron, gold and silver, but the rivers are mostly dry in summer, and lack of water is the great difficulty to be overcome. Still, strange to say, water can always be got a short distance below the surface, and at this season of the year—in July, August and September—there are incessant thunderstorms in the mountains, with tropical downpours of rain, which cut up and erode some parts of the country in an extraordinary manner.

We had an example of this on approaching Santa Fé. Our route lay along an arroya or dry river-bed, and a severe storm was raging not far away. Suddenly we heard a noise of rushing water, and a great torrent with a head like a Severn bore came down, cutting up the channel and carrying away the willows on the banks, and had it lasted long enough it would have spread over the plains and destroyed the crops.

One storm on Saturday week destroyed eight miles of railway in Southern Colorado. It was repaired and opened for traffic yesterday (Monday) for the first time, and they had to lay a completely new line, so effaced and cut up was the original track. I never saw anything like it.

These are the difficulties with which New Mexico has to

contend, situated as it is between the main ridge of the Rocky Mountains and the Sierra Nevada.

The heat was not oppressive, but here it is frightful again, and I long to be *en route* for San Francisco.

We start to-morrow morning at 7.0 from Denver, and reach San Francisco at 6 p.m. on Saturday.

I hope we shall escape being robbed on the way, as D. Wedderburn nearly was last year. We were followed by two men on Sunday night, crossing the Raton Pass into Trinidad, and the driver informed us that we should probably be robbed!

Fortunately, however, if the men were "road-agents," the darkness saved us, for they couldn't tell how many we were. Had they known that two of the passengers were women, and the fourth a boy, perhaps they would have stopped us.

Extract from Letter from Major Price

S.S. "DAKOTA" BETWEEN SAN FRANCISCO
AND VICTORIA, B.C.
September 12, 1878.

We reached San Francisco on Saturday the 7th of September and put up at the Palace Hotel, said to be the largest hotel in the world. After roughing it in New Mexico, and after the four days' journey from Denver, we were not sorry for this return to civilization, where we could feast off Californian delicacies and drink Californian wines *ad libitum*. The season in San Francisco has hardly commenced, and most of the people are at the various watering-places in North and South California, or in the mountains, to avoid the wind, dust, and fog of San Francisco.

The sun is very hot every morning, but about 2 o'clock the sea breeze comes, in rolls the fog, and the temperature falls 15° or 20° at once.

All over the valley there is nothing but sunlight and dust, with the fresh breeze in the afternoon to make the climate agreeable, and the country is covered with vineyards and orchards and orange groves, which supply the only green to relieve the monotony of the yellow stubble-fields and burnt pastures. Rain never falls except in spring.

I am told the vineyards are becoming very productive, and the wines, though rather strong, are of excellent flavour. The fruit goes all over America, but the apples and pears are very flavourless. I find little change in San Francisco. It is a long, straggling town, covering a number of steep hills, and occupying the slopes and valleys between.

It seems to be extending, but the houses are chiefly of wood, except in the principal streets. However, one has only to spend half an hour in the place to see that it is one of the busiest and richest cities in America.

Extract from Letter from Major Price.

VICTORIA, B.C.
Friday, September 13, 1878.

Reached Esquimalt this morning about 12.0 and drove at once to Victoria—about three miles.

There is a fairly good hotel here, kept by a Frenchman, and we have good quarters. Victoria is a curious place, a long, straggling town, built of wood.

The scenery is very picturesque, or would be if one could see it, but the bush and forests are on fire everywhere, and the smoke, mingling with the fog, covers the whole district with an impenetrable veil. The harbour and bays are very full, studded with islands, and covered with firs and pines to the water's edge.

I have met a very nice fellow here, Judge Crease, Chief Justice of the Province, and have just been to call.

He can't ask us to dinner, as they can't get servants, but we are going up this morning.

(*The travellers recrossed the continent by the route followed on the outward journey, visiting New York and Washington before sailing for England.*)

Part Three

IMPRESSIONS OF AMERICA
UNDER THE NEW DEAL

By M. PHILIPS PRICE, M.P., M.A., F.R.G.S.

CONTENTS: Part III

VI. ACROSS PRAIRIE AND PLATEAU. P. 140

Physico-Economic Divisions of North America—Across the Prairies of Nebraska—The Ranching System and its Future—We reach Colorado—Visit to a Ranch Settlement—Soil Erosion and the Advance of the Desert—We enter the Rockies—Through the Mining Camps—Company on a Trans-continental Train—The Plateaux of Utah—We arrive at Salt Lake City—Scenes of Mormon Life—Mormon Religion Today—The Political Campaign in Salt Lake City—We Cross the Salt Lake by Rail—A Glimpse of the Ranching State of Nevada.

VII. CALIFORNIA AND THE PACIFIC COAST. P. 152

First Impressions of San Francisco—The Problem of the Far East—Scenes in Chinatown—Class and Racial Complexities in California—Berkeley University—California, Creator of Hothouse Growths—We witness Upton Sinclair's Campaign—We visit Fruit Farms—Californian Fruit Growers' Problems—We visit the Giant Redwood Forests—A Civil Conservation Camp—Pacific Coast Scenes.

VIII. NATIONAL PARKS, LOS ANGELES AND THE GRAND CAÑON. P. 165

We visit the Yosemite Valley—Scenes in the National Park—Modern Luxury Travel—The American Genius for National Parks—Cosmopolitanism in Los Angeles—Waiting on the Films —A Talk with a German Immigrant—We cross the Arizona Desert—A Visit to the Grand Cañon—Nature's Sacrament!—Geological Causes—Scenes from an Indian Watch-Tower.

IX. NEW MEXICO—THE SPANISH-INDIAN FRINGE. P. 176

Wayside Scenes in New Mexico—An Indian Village—A Spanish Town—Scenes in Santa Fé—Spanish Society and Dancing—Spanish Culture and the Political Problems of New Mexico—Soil Erosion and the Indians—A Mexican Cowboy Village—We visit a Pueblo Indian Village—Indian Self-Government—Dual Religion of the Indians—America's Red Aristocrats—The Problem of the Rising Generation of the Indians—Mexican Religious Emigrants in U.S.A.

86

PREFACE TO PART III

THE following pages are based on letters written home, and on diaries and notes made during a three months' journey across the American continent in the autumn of 1934, on which I was accompanied by my wife. I covered as far as possible the route followed by my father, who made two journeys across the continent, sixty and fifty years ago, and wrote accurate diaries of what he saw. It therefore occurred to me that it would be interesting to compare the United States of the 'seventies with the country as it is to-day. My main objective was to study the New Deal, more particularly in its agricultural aspects, and for this reason we made only a short stay in the Eastern States, where the majority of travellers get their only impression of America. Most of our time was spent off the beaten track, in the Middle Western prairies, the plateaux of the Rockies, the valleys of California, the deserts of Arizona, and the cotton-fields of the South. In this way we were able to study the reactions of the people in the remoter States towards the big changes which have been initiated since President Roosevelt succeeded Mr. Hoover at the White House. But we also did a certain amount of sight-seeing, and some of the following pages describe wayside scenes and aspects of the countryside.

We were fortunate enough to witness the November elections of 1934, and to see something of the American political machine in action. But it must be remembered that much of what is written in the following pages must be read in the light of the situation existing in the country in the autumn of 1934. Many things have happened since then, and in May 1935 the United States Supreme Court uttered its fateful verdict on the New Deal.

M. P. P.

FIRST IMPRESSIONS:
NEW YORK AND CONNECTICUT

THE R.M.S. *Olympic* steamed up the Hudson River to Battery Point on the evening of October 2, 1934. As we passed the Statue of Liberty I recalled the gibe of Bernard Shaw—that upon this statue the words should be inscribed: "All hope abandon ye who enter here!" I instinctively revolted against such an interpretation of what we might be going to see in America. But as an antidote to the over-confident optimism so prevalent in America before the slump, the gibe was perhaps not out of place.

I hoped to find an answer to the question: What does the Statue of Liberty stand for today? It had a meaning which none could mistake when the French sculptor designed it many years ago. Then it stood in the eyes of immigrants from Europe for freedom from the cramped life on small farms and in old factories, freedom from military service to despots and oligarchs. It stood for prospects of boundless opportunity, on rich and unoccupied land, and work for high, if uncertain, wages. There were prospects for a man with health, strength and initiative. In a word, the Statue of Liberty stood for that new freedom for which Washington fought in 1776 and which Lincoln wrote in blood and tears in 1861–65.

But of one thing I was already convinced before we landed. The Statue of Liberty does not stand for that kind of liberty today. Liberty to come and go as you please may mean, in practice, liberty to starve. The immigration officers who came on board were a proof that the old liberty of movement into the great continent is a thing of the past—

and rightly so. The continent can no longer be the dumping-ground of those who merely seek liberty of movement and a better living than they can find in Europe. The movement and re-settlement of populations must be planned in this modern age. And it is to the advantage of the would-be immigrant that this should be so. For the Great Republic has new domestic problems. The passage of time compels a new interpretation for the Statue of Liberty.

These reflections were forgotten on landing. I was overwhelmed by my impressions of this greatest of American seaports. Looking at the sky-scrapers that surround Wall Street, the Empire State Building, and the great mansions that line Fifth Avenue, I was reminded of the film, *Metropolis*, which I saw some seven or eight years ago. Here was the nerve-centre of a vast industrial civilization, concentrated on this narrow tongue of land between the East and West Hudson River, revealing itself in tier upon tier of towering buildings, and vistas of narrow streets overhung by pinnacles of mounting masonry. Here in New York we seemed to see for the first time a new type of architecture emerging. Individually the buildings are not so imposing, though the massive power of some is touched with grace. But it is mainly their cumulative effect which makes one perceive New York as the climax of an age of industrial, commercial and financial concentration. London has room, in spite of its ground landlords, to expand. So has picturesque Paris and patriarchally planned Berlin. But New York has had to concentrate the trade and finance of one of the great continents of the earth into a few square miles of marsh on the River Hudson. Hence the need of a new type of architecture became imperative.

But is the great city built on sure foundations? Physically, yes. But economically? The wharves, two-thirds of which were empty, along the West Hudson and New Jersey shore, were eloquent of the catastrophe that had befallen the continent, as it has befallen the whole world—the paralysis of international trade. The sky-scrapers were built by the Trusts and Corporations when Wall Street was convinced that America was not only a land of boundless opportunity, but also one of perpetual prosperity. Many of them are half empty today. Will history see New York as a Colossus with feet of clay? It will surely do so if the United States does not play its part in a revival of international trade. If the country withdraws into its shell and becomes entirely self-supporting, in response to the suicidal urge that seems to have afflicted the whole world, its economic centre of gravity will shift away from the ports and industries of the East Coast to the centres round the Great Lakes and the plains of the Mississippi.

I was soon aware of the social problem in New York. Between the wharves on the one side and the massive business metropolis on the other lies the belt of the dock labourers' quarters. Living in red brick tenement-houses, provided with ugly, if useful, fire-escapes in the form of external stairways, these people are of every type and race and nationality that Europe has produced. Some have been completely Americanized in the melting-pot, some only half assimilated. Only when a second generation has passed through the American schools is process complete. Then the only reminder of European origin is the surname, and perhaps the religion. Probably half these people are now unemployed or frozen-in, a derelict population, unwanted until such time as international trade revives. Meanwhile they have to be fed, and it is to the credit of President Roosevelt that he was the first great leader to organize the relief of these submerged social elements as a Federal public service, and to help the municipalities and States of the Union to cope with these new obligations. The Statue of

Liberty already has a new meaning. Liberty has begun to acquire a social conscience.

We saw a little of the negro population in Haarlem. Some of the negroes are unskilled dock labourers, others are shop-keepers and middle-class types, some of them fairly well-to-do. One notices a good many yellow and "high yellow" people, and receives the impression that here at least a slow process of absorption of the black race by the white is proceeding; but the black element is constantly renewed by fresh immigrants from the South in search of casual labour. Whether this immigration will continue now, in view of the immense reduction of oversea trade, is doubtful. It is possible that the movement of the coloured peoples into centres like New York will rapidly decline, and that the absorption of the coloured elements remaining in the North would make bigger inroads upon racial purity than has hitherto been the case. I heard the view expressed by more than one American in New York that this would be the ultimate solution of the coloured question, at all events in the North. I was struck by the absence of any outward sign of racial feeling, although I understand that it does break out at times. The school-teachers with whom I spoke seemed to be doing their utmost to make things easy for the small proportion of negro children who attend white schools in districts where the races are mixed. They described the standard of intelligence of the negro children as being only slightly below that of the white child. This may be due to environmental as well as racial factors. I got the impression that the North American does not waste sentiment on the negro, nor does he pretend to love him. But he does accord him equal rights, and, up to a point, equal opportunities. In fact, he tries as far as possible to carry out the spirit and letter of the American Constitution as it affects the two races.

During our stay in New York I paid several visits to Wall Street. I found the bankers and stock-brokers in an unhappy and unchastened mood. They seemed to have learnt nothing and forgotten nothing. They feel that the New Deal is a dangerous experiment and that they will have to pay for it. They ignored the fact that the Federal Government saved them when it closed the banks for a few days in the panic of 1933, and restored the public confidence which they had destroyed. They are willing to accept that species of aid, but unwilling to give any kind of guarantee that the same sort of trouble will not occur again. They talked as if they wanted Roosevelt to abandon public relief schemes for giving work to the unemployed, and in return they had nothing to offer save cut-throat competition and the old unplanned speculation. They are the modern American Bourbons. Wall Street still has a long way to go before it begins to think in terms of social planning, and probably many of the old leaders will be gone before this happens, unless a storm of public indignation sweeps away the whole system. If this does happen one can only hope that the New Deal will be far enough advanced to put something in its place, or chaos will ensue.

At the same time, one must recognize that Wall Street is a product of tradition. The American public has always been liable to crises of speculative fever. The atmosphere of the frontier and the rôle of the pioneer encourage speculation and discourage investment. 50 per cent of the Federal Government Bonds are held by the banks, and 50 per cent are in the hands of the investing public. In England not more than 25 per cent of Government stocks are held by the banks. Britain has a much larger investing public than the United States. The Englishman usually divides his investments between the speculative and the gilt-edged, and he consequently stands more firmly on his feet. The American stock-holder does not, which probably accounts for the severity of the American slumps. Another thing that struck me about the Wall Street mentality (and I observed the same thing later on among industrial leaders in New England and the West) was the inordinate fear of any sort of public expenditure. I found the brokers excitedly discussing principles which all political parties have long ago accepted in England. It seemed to them intolerable that public money should be spent to relieve destitution or provide work for the unemployed. They talked as if national bankruptcy was staring the country in the face. Yet the fact remains that the national indebtedness of the United States up to December 31, 1934, was 382 dollars per head of population against 967 dollars in Great Britain. Even if the President spends all the money that Congress has allowed him to spend up to June 1936, this debt will still remain at less than half the British figure. The inordinate fear betrayed by business men in the States of any public expenditure of money seems to me largely traditional. The American business man and financial leader simply cannot conceive that the State should intervene to alleviate a grave social evil. Hitherto private enterprise has been allowed so to dominate everything that a failure of private enterprise simply cannot be imagined.

A visit to the journalists and editors of the more radical newspapers and periodicals convinced me that these had no good word to say about President Roosevelt and the New Deal, but for precisely the opposite reasons to those obtaining in Wall Street. The latter talked as if Roosevelt were a Communist, the former as if he were a Fascist. Generally speaking, as far as I could learn, New York had very little sympathy with the Roosevelt Administration. But the critics cancelled one another out. Such supporters of the New Deal as I met were mostly people who seemed to have some link with the Administration. I suspected that their motives were not disinterested, and that the prospect of jobs had something to do with their sympathy. Many young intellectuals, however, seem recently to have "gone Left." Radical books were prominently displayed, even in Fifth Avenue. But the fact that Mr. Du Pont's son had gone Communist, and that John Strachey's *Struggle for Power* had sold well, was of less significance, to my thinking, than the political allegiance of the average New York mechanic and dock labourer. In spite of all the clamour of the reactionaries and revolutionaries, I believe the average New Yorker, though puzzled, is prepared to give the President a chance for the next year or two. New York, like all large metropolitan cities, is apt to become a sounding-board for extremes. The crowded and noisy atmosphere of the city seems to accentuate this tendency.

From October the 6th to the 8th we were staying on a small holding in Cornwall County, Connecticut. Our host was a week-ender, who, with a number of other business and professional men, had formed a co-operative week-end colony in a clearing of the wooded Connecticut hills. In a central farmhouse the colony kept a farmer and his wife, to provide them with dairy and poultry produce, and the different families were scattered about the hillside in picturesque wooden bungalows. Along the valley bottoms, as we motored from New York, we saw colonies of unemployed persons who have taken up derelict plots of land, and are growing vegetables or keeping poultry on small subsistence holdings. None of the New Deal agencies seemed to be helping them. They represented an unassisted natural growth of the surplus town population, spilling back into the countryside. They must find it a hard struggle to make ends meet without State assistance. Probably their savings, and assistance from relatives, have made these "new starts" possible. Connecticut was colonized by the pioneers in the early days of the Republic. These pioneers passed on across the mountains, to open up the plains of the Mississippi, leaving the Connecticut valleys derelict. Will these valleys be recolonized by the unemployed from the newly derelict seaport cities, seeking subsistence on the land?

We spent Sunday with a dairy farmer, the son of a man who was formerly wealthy, but was badly hit in the great depression. He had gone back to the land for a living, and was apparently making a success of it. The great cities of New England provide a great market for dairy and poultry produce, and evidently the type of farming is slowly changing, much as it is in the South of England. But I was struck by the much greater advance which has been made in respect of dairy herd management in America. Concerted action has been taken there to clean the herds of bovine tuberculosis, while nothing, or next to nothing, has been done in England. I found that in Connecticut, as in a great part of the United States as a whole, large areas were completely free of the disease. Reacting animals are removed from the herd, and compensation is paid, the farmer, the State and the Federal Government sharing the loss.

Another factor that seems to help the American dairy farmer is the public habit of drinking milk. Fresh milk is obtainable everywhere at meals, as easily as beer and spirits are obtainable in England. One misses in the United States the constant advertisements of brewery and distillery companies. The public is not always having beer and spirits rammed down its throat! Prohibition has at all events had some beneficial result—it has induced the public to take more kindly to milk.

I rode on horseback that Sunday afternoon, with a friend from the above-mentioned farm, through forested hills and valleys; a sea of crimson and gold as far as the eye could reach. Outside a little wooden church a large fleet of motor-cars was standing. A service was going on. Judging by the number of cars present, far more persons seemed to be attending church than one would find in the depth of rural England. On the way back to the week-end colony we passed the old colonial town of Lichfield, where before the Revolution there was a statue of George III. I was impressed by the grace and charm of the old wooden houses with their porches, verandas, and Corinthian columns, which might have seen George Washington riding by. Here Harriet Beecher Stowe lived and wrote her momentous novel. Here one was conscious of the old Puritan America and the shades of the Pilgrim Fathers.

CHAPTER II

NEW ENGLAND

ON October 17th we paid a visit to Gloucester (Massachusetts), founded originally by people from the English city of Gloucester, from which my own family comes. It was in 1869 that my father visited the place, then a little fishing community, bringing from my grandfather a painting of the parent city, as a present to Gloucester of the New World. The Mayor and Mayoress had had word of our arrival, and accorded us a welcome in keeping with the hospitality that met us wherever we went in the United States. It struck us at once that no Mayor of an English city would spend a whole day on entertaining two strangers, as did the Mayor of Gloucester and his wife. The place lives partly by fishing and the manufacture of fish products, and partly by providing week-ends and holidays for the business people of Boston. The population is heterogeneous in type. The business men and leaders of local opinion whom we met at the City Hall were mainly of the Anglo-Saxon stock. Most of them told us that their ancestors came originally from England, Scotland, or North Ireland, in the eighteenth or nineteenth century. When we were taken round to see the fish paste and glue factories we saw unskilled workers and artisans of Latin stock, mostly Portugese, Italian, and Spanish. Immigrants before the war, they were to some extent a separate community. I saw a Communist placard in one of the factories, and realized that radical ideas were held by some of the unskilled workers of Gloucester. There is a danger here that class feeling may be reinforced by race feeling, and even by religious differences. This would be unhealthy if local politics was at all corrupt.

But my impression was that here at least political life was clean and moderately progressive. There was no Irish element on the municipal council, no local Tammany. The middle class of Gloucester seemed fully aware of the social problems of the day. In the City Hall a staff of clerks was at work on the local administrative and relief problems. Their status seemed guaranteed. I did not gather that they were liable to lose their jobs if there was a change of Mayor. If this condition could prevail generally in the United States there might be some chance of creating an honest and efficient local civil service, which is badly needed at present. But here, in this small New England town, I seemed to see it in operation.

Another thing struck us most favourably. There was a complete absence of snobbery. A prominent lady in the town told us quite openly, in the presence of others, that she was a seamstress before her marriage. Indeed, she seemed proud of the fact that she had earned her living in this way. I thought of Gloucester in England. What lady prominent in local society there would boast that she had earned her living as a seamstress? This absence of snobbery is one of the best features of American society.

Gloucester (Mass.) seems typical of the small provincial towns in the United States, which are gradually creating a healthier atmosphere in local politics. Being a small and developing place, it has never had to contend with a local Tammany, or any kind of vested interest in its local government. The older and larger cities, like New York and Boston, have a class of politician and a boss system so firmly entrenched that it is almost impossible to effect a reform. But if industry becomes decentralized in accordance with the modern tendency, and if the smaller provincial towns continue to grow, a cleaner political atmosphere may arise in the new cities. Then what with the Federal administration, and an incorrupt provincial civil service in the smaller towns, the older cities could be left to themselves. But Tammany has already obtained a hold in some of the small provincial centres of New England. I found that in one place, during the worst of the slump, the school-teachers were not paid for over a year, because the local authority could not collect the revenue. So the Greek community, which largely controlled the local council, paid the teachers' salaries out of their own pockets. This dependence of a local authority on a racial community, which brings whole sections of the population into its debt, is one of the worst features of the Tammany system.

Our stay in New England was further enriched by a visit to the house of three American friends, two of whom we had met in Europe a few years before. They live in a charming villa in Longmeadow (Mass.). They were typical New England intellectuals, cultured Americans who were true to all the best traditions of their country, but at the same time sufficiently in touch with Europe, and even with the Far East, to be able to understand the outlook of the rest of the world. It is people of this type who will in time break down that tendency to isolation which has for so long been an American tradition. In this respect New England is in advance of the rest of the States, having a more liberal outlook on the world. It is mainly in this part of the continent that one meets with that fine type of humanity, the cultured North American who knows something of the rest of the world. One of our hosts lectures to New England audiences in the winter, and travels each summer to collect material. My wife and I accompanied her on a three days' lecture tour through Massachusetts.

One day during this tour we attended a social gathering at Wellesley Hills in a suburban villa, the property of a lawyer. Those present were the wives and daughters of typical professional and business men. I was struck by the immense vitality of the women, both here and on other occasions. Their interest in public affairs was most striking, and I don't think provincial women of the professional classes in England would have shown the intelligent interest manifested by this gathering at Wellesley Hills. On the other hand, I noticed that the American men whom we met at other functions betrayed less interest in public affairs than Englishmen of the same class. I had the impression that American men are so overworked, so absorbed in business and the struggle to make money, or rather to keep, by hook or by crook, what they already have, that they can find no time to think about the government of their country. American women, on the other hand, are so much freer from the drudgery of household work than English women, thanks to the hundred and one inventions and labour-saving devices that have been perfected in America, that they have time to devote to the study of public affairs. They read widely, and engage in intellectual pursuits, far more than do English women. I think the cold winters, and the difficulty of enjoying outdoor sports and exercise at certain times of the year, may be partly responsible. On the other hand, English women may have better complexions, thanks to our mild climate and our better aired houses. American houses are misery for a poor Englishman who is not used to living in an atmosphere like that of the palm-house of a botanical garden on a hot July day!

On our way back from Wellesley Hills to Longmeadow we dined at the old Wayside Inn, which has seen many historic persons within its walls. It was here that Emerson penned some of those lines of vigorous optimism which blended the New England intellect with the philosophy of the frontier and the Wild West.

Our next lecture tour took us to Albany and Troy, over a

part of the Berkshire hills. We were greatly struck by the beauty and well-planned style of the towns and villages through which we passed. We liked the wide streets and the adequate green spaces between the houses. These were mostly of wood, and I did not see quite the same difference between rich and poor, as regards the style of the houses, which is so apparent in England. It is not so easy to tell the difference between the working-class quarter, the smaller professional or bank clerk quarter, and the well-to-do residential quarter, as in an English provincial town. Snobbery is not legible in the architecture of American towns. Moreover, one misses the dreary rows of brick houses which made such an eyesore of much of Victorian England.

The forested valleys leading up to the Berkshires were interspersed with open spaces. On these scanty woodland meadows some small-holders were trying to eke out a living by keeping cows and goats and growing a few plots of maize. These were some of the settlers whom the depression had caught. Their ramshackle houses, messy little yards and lean cattle showed that they were hardly equal to their task. Not far away was a Federal Government Civil Conservation Camp, where unemployed men were working on the preservation and improvement of the forests. They seemed well-fed and contented, though doubtless the work is hard for those who are not used to it.

Arriving at Albany, the capital of New York State, we saw a large number of students in the streets and cafeterias. They were young men and women of the professional and middle classes, studying at the college and University. Rarely have I seen more earnest and intelligent faces. The girls were handsome, but again I missed the colour of the English complexion. If this is the younger generation of university students, it augurs well for the future of the

country. But will these young people find work when they
leave college? On that all depends. The European counter-
parts to these types have been the recruiting ground for
Fascism. In the neighbouring town of Troy, later in the day,
we heard a lecture on the Far East. About a hundred women
from middle-class homes listened attentively for over an
hour to a masterly plea for a sensible understanding between
the United States and Japan in respect of the problems of
Manchuria and China. Ten years ago these American
women would not have listened to a lecture which told them
that the United States and Japan have common interests
in world economic recovery. Conversation with some of the
audience at tea afterwards left me with the impression that
they were in an anxious and somewhat chastened mood as
regards the state of the world, and ready to listen to any new
idea.

Before I left England I had been given a letter of introduction from the head of one of our agricultural colleges to
Mr. Parmalee Prentice, who lives at Mount Hope near
Williamstown (Mass.). Soon after our arrival in New York
we had received a cordial invitation to come and spend a
week-end with him. We were prepared for the open-hearted
generosity which Americans always extend even to complete
strangers, but for what we experienced at Mount Hope we
were not prepared. We had expected to visit a small New
England country house with a farm attached, where experi-
ments in cattle-breeding were being carried on. To our
surprise we were driven up to a large country mansion of
red brick with marble columns, surrounded by acres and
acres of park. The drive was of perfect tarmacadam, and it
seemed that every leaf was swept from it by gangs of
gardeners. A giant Stars and Stripes fluttered in the breeze
on the front lawn, whence we had a fine view of the rolling
Berkshire hills, a blaze of orange and golden autumn tints.

We were cordially received by Mr. and Mrs. Prentice, and found the interior of the house no less sumptuous than the outside. There were lifts up to each landing, bathrooms in each room, and also telephones, an electric organ to play us hymns on Sunday morning before breakfast, and a fresh set of crockery and silver for each meal. We then realized that we were in the home of one of America's millionaires, and that our hostess was a daughter of John D. Rockefeller (sen.).

Next morning Mr. Prentice took us to visit his farms and animal-breeding stations. I would gladly have walked, being that troublesome creature, an Englishman, who likes to shake up his liver and get a warm glow in his body. But nothing doing! A fleet of cars, with chauffeurs, was ready to take us to our destination, though this was less than a mile away.

Mr. Prentice has been working at a method of breeding bulls to improve the yield of milk of dairy cattle. A cursory glance at his records showed that he had met with considerable success. He had employed at his own expense some first-rate biologists and experts in Genetics. Starting with an average commercial dairy cow, he had worked a herd up to milk yields of astronomic heights. One wonders what sort of a cow he will turn out if he goes on. In his poultry-houses one saw hens which had never set foot on the earth, but lived all their lives in wire cages. Mr. Prentice's vision of the future seemed to be that of animal food-factories of colossal efficiency; and perhaps he is right. But then the Middle Western farmers and ranchers will all be on relief, and the wild prairies will roll back over the last vestige of human activity, while all America's food will be produced in the animal factories of New England. Mr. Prentice rightly believes in Science as the great liberator of Mankind. He maintains that in agriculture, as well as in industry, it can reduce the costs of production and the price of food to the consumer, and thereby indirectly raise wages. But as we talked next morning at breakfast over our grapefruit and corn-cakes, he refused to admit my contention that what he was doing was to create an immense social problem. Scientific devices, saving labour and wages, would cause social dislocation, and social effort and reorganization would be needed to re-establish equilibrium. Hours must be shortened, real wages must be raised, and the capital operating these processes must be controlled. This he vehemently denied. But our talks were good fun. He probably thought me a crazy Englishman with Socialistic European ideas. For my part, I recognized him as an American Henry Ford in agriculture, doing excellent work as far as it goes, but failing to see that in the twentieth century individual effort is not enough. We left Mount Hope with a feeling that if all wealthy Americans used their wealth for the advancement of scientific knowledge, as Mr. Prentice has done, the type would be more popular.

Returning to Longmeadow on October 21st, I went that Sunday morning to hear a service at the Congregational Church in Springfield, conducted by a well-known preacher. My first impression of the service was one of amazement. It was fortunate that I was early, or I should not have found even standing-room. Being used as I am to seeing half-empty and even almost completely empty churches in England, I began to realize that the churches in America really do seem to play an important part in helping to mould public opinion. Dr. Gilkie is, of course, a well-known preacher, and therefore something of a "draw," but I noticed on other Sundays also that the churches were far fuller than in England. I was particularly struck by the number of young people I saw there. Another thing that impressed me was the fact that the method of conducting the service was in the full sense of the word popular and even unconventional. The preacher began his sermon with an address to the children. He brought an alarm-clock into the pulpit, informing the children that he had picked it up on a rubbish-heap, and that the clock had told him that it had been thrown away by its owner because it did not go off when required, was unreliable, and did not speak the truth. He had taken pity on it, and had decided to give it a fresh chance. He had set it to go off just at that moment. Would it mend its ways and be reliable? The whole congregation sat as still as mice. One could have heard a pin drop. As the silence continued, and it became clear that the clock would not speak the truth, a titter was heard, then a guffaw, and then a peal of laughter, until finally the whole congregation rocked and the church re-echoed with mirth. I saw then why the churches in America are full on Sundays. I think, however, there is another reason as well. In England the churches have not until recently concerned themselves much with social questions. They have confined themselves to matters of individual morality, and the personal relations of one man to another. The relations of each man and woman to society, and the problems of social organization, they have left alone. The political parties have dealt with these matters, and public life in England is sufficiently clean to enable them to give tolerable satisfaction in their treatment of these questions. But as I have said, in America all the ablest men avoid politics and go into private business or the churches. The political parties are organizations enabling certain people to make a living. The churches therefore have not had to reckon with the competition of the political parties in focussing attention on social problems. And I noted that questions of housing and public relief and education were being discussed by the young people's clubs which are organized in connection with the churches. I suspect that these church bodies do more social thinking than the local caucuses of the Republican and Democratic parties.

On the evening of October 21st, we went to a dinner-party in Longmeadow, before we set out on our trek across the continent. We met business men, school-teachers, women who were social workers, professional people, and even one or two ladies and gentlemen at large, who had seen the world, and represented the cultured New Englander. It was, I think, a fairly representative gathering of provincial New England. The conversation was far more witty and vivacious than it would have been at a similar gathering in England. I was continually conscious of the volcanic energy which distinguishes the American people, and which found expression in the conversation. No precedent or convention stands in the way of a clean sweep, a "big idea," if experience shows that it is necessary. The only question asked is: Will it work? The brilliant talk, and the warm air of the overheated house, reminded me of the sort of atmosphere that I had known in Russia. The American climate is like the Russian in its extremes of heat and cold, and doubtless makes for vivacity and mental activity. And yet I felt that the Americans are far nearer to us than to the Russians. They and we have a common Anglo-Saxon culture; we speak the same language, and we both believe in free speech, in open discussion, in counting heads instead of breaking them. In both countries the policeman exists for us and not we for him. But in the United States two opposing influences are at work. The climate and the physical atmosphere tend to produce outbursts of activity, followed by periods of relaxation. As in Russia, they would normally be conducive to long phases of inactivity, followed by revolutionary outbreaks. But America got its early traditions and cultural influences from the democracies of Western Europe, French and Anglo-Saxon, and these have so far resisted the natural climatic tendency toward the mental reactions of the Slavs. In the meantime they have helped to create that most valuable and interesting phenomenon, the American temperament, the product of West European culture and the American climate.

CHAPTER III

NIAGARA AND DETROIT

WE reached Buffalo on the morning of October 22nd, arriving by the night train from Springfield, and arranged for a day's visit to Niagara Falls by car. After seeing the Falls from the American side we crossed the Niagara River into Canada, and visited the Canadian side. We noticed one thing during our passage from American to Canadian territory and back. It may seem a small thing, but little straws often indicate great currents. On passing the Canadian frontier we found the officials very polite and deferential. They even touched their caps on examining our passports. On our return to the States we were greeted with such questions as: "Where are you people from?" And the officials, with tunic half undone, would saunter out, chewing gum and spitting. They were not rude, but simply very informal. Now this, I think, is typical of a certain very important difference between the United States and the British Dominion. The difference is in some degree flattering to and in some degree a criticism of each country. It shows the strength in the United States of the ultra-democratic ideal—the motion that all men are born equal. At the same time, the public cannot feel much respect for State officials who behave so informally.—On the other hand, in Canada we find something of the British tradition of deference on the part of the official to the public that he serves. The danger here is that deference may degenerate into the snobbishness from which the United States is so free.

On October 23rd we reached Detroit by the night train from Buffalo, and went straight to Dearborn, where Henry Ford has his great motor works, and where a regular satellite town has grown up round an industry—a proof of the modern tendency towards decentralization. Dearborn has its own civic life, quite separate from that of Detroit, which remains a huge industrial city, but is under the direction, as far as its local government is concerned, of its own Tammany, in which, as usual, the Irish Catholic element is predominant. I have remarked before that the one hope of breaking the power of Tammany throughout the United States probably lies in the growth of satellite towns round decentralized industries. But here in Dearborn there is another problem. From the frying-pan of Tammany one jumps into the fire of the industrial paternalism of Henry Ford. Fordism, judged by book-keeping standards, may be more efficient than Tammany, but will it permit of the development of individual liberty and happiness, and of a civic consciousness? Dearborn is really run by an industrial oligarchy centred on the person of Henry Ford. Their will determines the lives and welfare of all the inhabitants. There can be no independent thinking under these conditions, because there is no organ of free opinion. It is an industrial Tsardom, albeit of a most efficient and benevolent kind, but a Tsardom for all that.

Dearborn is a sort of mass-production workshop, museum, and scientific laboratory combined. Every comfort is provided for the visitor, in the form of a special hotel. We spent the morning in the museum, and saw the scientific laboratory from the outside. The exhibits are all housed in magnificent buildings, some in Tudor, some in Queen Anne style. There is apparently nothing original about the architecture favoured by the American industrial magnates. In the main the architects follow the classical models of Europe. In the museum Ford has the beginnings of a wonderful permanent exhibition of articles designed to show how transport and industry have developed down the ages, from the caveman's tool to the aeroplane and the motor-car. Outside, in the park-like grounds, there are steamers and boats from early times floating on the lakes. There are examples of houses, shops, and village industries, which show how the habits of man have changed with the growth of scientific discovery and improved methods of transport. As you move from place to place in the park, old-fashioned coaches drive up and take you where you want to go. We saw Henry Ford himself walking about with some visitors. He seemed amazingly active and well for a man of over seventy. His whole life is now devoted to perfecting this great museum, a monument to himself and to his great hero and inspirer, Thomas Edison.

The most significant thing I saw that morning was the inscription over the main entrance to the scientific laboratory. It ran: "Man's Progress takes place over a Bridge built by the Agriculturalist, the Engineer and the Scientist." This is the key to Ford's philosophy, but it is, of course, nothing new. The whole of the Russian Revolution is based on this theory, and writers, from poor, dreary, old Karl Marx down to H. G. Wells, have been preaching it for the last eighty years. Ford's special contribution to this philosophy has been his sincere attempt to bring the fruits of invention down to the consuming masses, while still preserving the profit-motive of industry known as capitalism. The claims of the consumer on the product of industry and production for use rather than for profit have constituted the Socialist case for decades. If Ford can benefit the consumer and also produce for profit, he may save the capitalist system, which is probably why the Russian Bolsheviks respect and to a certain extent fear him. Cheap mass-production, with the main eye on the consumer, presupposes, if a certain amount of profit is still to be allowed to the managers, a high degree of planning. Ford does not love profit-seekers and investors.

But his weakness is that he does not realize the social effect of his cheap mass-production, which can only be remedied by social services, shorter hours, and guaranteed earnings. In other words, the State must take a hand. The benevolent industrial autocrat will not be able to put the world right without the work of the social planner. The fruits of industry cannot be brought to the masses by cheap production alone. Social services must be organized as a channel through which they must pass. Yet Mr. Ford thunders against social services, and in this respect proves himself no better than the average Wall Street obscurantist, a type which, in other respects, he heartily dislikes.

In the afternoon we visited the main workshops where the mass-production of cars is effected. Rows of men stand beside the conveyers, and as the components pass each man has his particular job—to bore a hole, fit a pin, or tighten a nut. At the end of the conveyers the parts are collected and placed near the chassis of a car. One large conveyer moves the chassis along, and from the end of the long shed, in about forty minutes' time, the complete car is driven off the premises. In this way 1,800 cars a day were being turned out when we were at Dearborn. In the boom years the output was 3,000 cars. The unskilled men were getting five dollars a day, and the skilled workers more. We could see that the pressure of work must be very great. The conveyers were keyed up to the pace of the average man, and woe to those who could not keep up with it. I heard from many sources that some men cannot stand the strain after five years at the conveyer. Moreover, there is no guarantee of earnings, even of a low minimum. In spite of all his ideas of keeping up buying power by cheap production, Ford was obliged, in the depression, to cut production and dismiss workers. Hundreds of men earned the high wage of five dollars a day for a couple of months, and then starved for the remaining ten. Until there is a guaranteed minimum for the year, or some scheme of unemployment insurance, run either by the State, or by the firm, all Ford's benevolent despotism must fail to solve the gravest of our modern social problems. In spite of the many interesting and wonderful things which we saw on our visit to Dearborn, I was not swept off my feet, nor did I fail to see that with all our slowness we in England have a sounder social basis in our systems of insurance and public service. If these could be welded to the practical idealism of Henry Ford, the world might indeed be a better place.

CHAPTER IV

CHICAGO

MY first impressions of Chicago, where we arrived on October 24th, were definitely pleasing. The waterfront along the shores of Lake Michigan offered a striking spectacle. Chicago has more room to be impressive than New York. It is not confined to a narrow tongue of land, but is able to sprawl along the lake shores. The admirably conducted tours round the city give one a good idea of all that a foreign traveller is expected to see of the polished exterior of this great city, whose population exceeds four millions. The flats of the millionaires, with special lifts which hoist their motor-cars to bedrooms behind their masters' apartments, and the exclusive clubs, which none but a few families can enter, show that a section, I think a small section, of the American public is trying to forget its lowly origins and imitate the snobbery of old England. Money indeed has beautified the lake front of Chicago. It has forced back the waters of the lake, and made fine parks arise in their place. The Elks' War Memorial, and a beautiful piece of sculpture in the park, near the University, depicting the Ages of Man in stone, as Shakespeare once depicted them in words, show that Chicago's artistic sense is alive, if not particularly original. We were greatly impressed by the University students who accompany the tourists, in order to earn money during their vacations. They are fine specimens of modern American youth. They avoid the coarse jokes and facetious remarks so usual with the old type of conductor, and really concentrate on giving the tourist a reliable account of the history, social life and art of their city.

One of the first things we did after our arrival was to visit the World Fair. We were lucky enough to get there just a week before it closed down for ever after a run of two years. It had been organized to illustrate a century of development in North America. On the surface, at least, it succeeded in exhibiting a certain kind of development. It was exceedingly imposing. It extended for nearly two miles along the lake shore, and almost all the chief industries on the continent of North America were represented. It certainly showed what its promoters set out to show—a century of progress. But what kind of progress? The great motor firms told the same story that Ford was telling in his private exhibition at Dearborn—progress effected by scientific invention, and by keeping such troublesome things as an interfering Government and a social conscience in the background; in short, Science and Rugged Individualism. And I admit that the scientific side of the show was most impressive. We twice saw *The Wings of a Century*, a pageant acted on the lake shore, demonstrating the progress of transport from the days of the buffaloes and the Indians to the days of the "Twentieth Century Limited," with the actual vehicles employed, from the Erie Canal barge and the old wood-burning steam engine to the super-heated express locomotive and the Transcontinental Streamliner. Without doubt the Chicago Fair showed one that man can produce great instruments of transport and production. But we knew that before, and the crowd from the back-streets of Chicago knew it, for they seemed more interested in the side-shows. After all, these inventions had brought no happiness to them. The Science Building, however, seemed very popular and was patronized by students and people of the middle class from all over the States and Canada, who were really thrilled by the photo-electric cell and the hidden mysteries of the atom. There was also a pleasing exhibit of the more modern types of architecture, buildings characterized by straight lines and broad surfaces. But I think the palm must be awarded to the exhibit of the Federal Government. Perhaps it was possible to see them in other parts of the Fair, and perhaps I missed them there, but it was only in the Federal Government building that I saw the things that really matter in the twentieth century. In the rest of the Fair I saw the things that really mattered in the nineteenth century. I don't know if the advent of the Roosevelt Administration was at all responsible for this, but it was clear that Washington was alive to what the public mind should be focussed on. In the Government building I saw how the Western farmer can grapple with the problem of soil erosion, the legacy of decades of ruthless exploitation of Mother Earth; how the national forests can be preserved and forest belts planted across the prairies; what improvements have been made in the material and moral welfare of the wage-earning class, and what further progress is needed; what a potential market there is for the unsaleable surplus of American agriculture, if only the people have more money to buy. One could go on writing endlessly of the impressions of this great Fair, which, with all its tendency to loiter in the past, showed a definite understanding of the problems of the future. Judging by what I heard, this change of attitude had come about in the last year through pressure exerted by public-spirited people, and, judging by the Federal Government's exhibit, through pressure from Washington.

On our last day at the Fair, three days before it closed for good, I examined an exhibit of a house made of a patent wood preparation and built in sections, so that it could be taken down and transported from place to place whenever the owner wanted to move. I remembered a letter written by my father from Chicago in 1869, in which he spoke of having seen a Chicago family moving its wooden house on rollers to a new site. Since then Chicago had been burnt down and rebuilt. On the Lake front rose the great villas and palaces of the millionaires, many of them empty since the slump. In the back areas, west of the river, had risen the slums. Was this movable modern house a shadow of things to come? Would the twentieth century Chicagoan, stranded in the great city by the depression and change of circumstances, take up his house and move away to new employment in the distant provinces, where industry is being decentralized? In my father's day the population of Chicago was rising by leaps and bounds. Last year, I understand, for the first time it showed a decline. The wings of the nineteenth century carried Chicago to Olympian heights. The wings of the twentieth century may have another destination for it—not perhaps up in the clouds, but on more solid ground, and on a firmer foundation.

On our second day at Chicago I visited the famous stockyards. These are enormous establishments on the outskirts of the city. About five great meat trusts have their killing, dressing and packing stations there. Roughly 700 pigs an hour are killed in one of these places alone, and 150 oxen. I saw the pigs being driven into an enclosure in which there is a great wheel. A negro slings a cord round the hind-leg of one animal, and the wheel draws it up until it is suspended on a chain and slowly conveyed down the line. "Round goes the wheel to the music of the Squeal." A man with a knife sticks the pig as it passes, another singes its hair, a score of others dress the carcase, others cut it up, and within a quarter of an hour a live pig is converted into hams and bacon ready for curing. I saw the beeves treated in much the same manner, except that they are first stunned with the poleaxe and then stuck.

We were taken through acres and acres of store-houses, stockyards, and chemical laboratories, where the enormous number of by-products coming from the animals are tested. Lard, soap, and floor polish, to say nothing of every conceivable kind of prepared foods, are handled by these firms. One could not fail to be impressed by the enormous concentrated power of the capital that controls these animal products, which has the Western farmer absolutely at its mercy. I noticed that some of the independent farmers' political organizations, now active in Wisconsin and Michigan, were beginning to talk about the nationalization of the packing corporations. Some people, in fact, were talking Socialism without mentioning the word. Nobody bothers about political theory in America, and perhaps this is just as well. But trusts and powerful corporations were never popular with the Western farmer. These enormous private vested interests have grown up at the centre where the nerve-fibres of the agricultural Middle West and the industrial East meet.

The phenomenal growth of Chicago dates from the Civil War, when the old patriarchal, self-supporting farming families, who worked their land by manual labour, were broken up by the drafts of the young men to the Union armies. The Chicago manufacturer saw his chance in this crisis, and pushed his labour-saving machinery across the newly-built railways to the farms, where the women and old men raised and harvested the crops with half the expenditure of time and energy. It was Chicago and the industrialized Middle West that finally crushed the South, and enabled Grant to steam-roller the Confederate armies, which not even the brilliance of Robert E. Lee could hold together. From that time dates Chicago's dominance over the Middle West, as manifested in these great packing plants, which handle almost everything that the farmer wants to buy or sell. No wonder the Middle Western farmer is liable to bouts of rebellion against the corporations, as witness Bryan's "Cross of Gold," and Theodore Roosevelt's

"Trust-busters," and more recently Governor Olsen's Farmers Labour Party, to say nothing of La Follette's rule in Michigan.

On our third day in Chicago I presented a letter of introduction to the Chief Commissioner of Police. As I had expected, I found that he and many of his assistants were Irish, and visions of Tammany Hall floated before my eyes. I had heard a lot of unsavoury stories about the connection between the gangster world and the city government of Chicago, and I knew the reputation of all the larger cities in States as regards local government. But whatever may have been going on behind the scenes, we were impressed by the efficiency with which the Police Department of Chicago is run. The Irish may have a bad record of graft and corruption in the States, but we received the impression that there has been a clean-up in Chicago since the abolition of Prohibition, and it may be hoped that the atmosphere has become permanently purer. Certainly the Irish heads of the Chicago Police did not appear as though they wanted to hide anything from us. They admitted that things had been very bad, but they insisted that the city was turning over a new leaf, and that the gangsters were really on the run. Things had come to such a pass that shortly before Prohibition ended the gangsters were running the liquor and the white slave traffic, squaring the police, terrorizing the City Council, and murdering all those who dared to raise their voices against them. Now, it seemed, the tables were being turned. There was no need for foreign police to point to Chicago as a warning. On the other hand, Scotland Yard had just sent someone over to get hints on traffic management from the Chicago police. We met in the Deputy Chief's office a Police Commissioner from Chile who had come to study American methods. And we found that modern science was being used to defeat the gangster. We were proudly shown the room which was the nerve-centre of the telephone and radio connection between the public, reporting attacks or robberies, and the police cars, fitted with radio apparatus and cruising in all sections of the city and suburbs. We were there when a message came in to the effect that a robbery had taken place in a certain street. At once an order was sent out by wireless to Car No. so-and-so, to proceed to a certain spot, investigate, and report. Generally the car is on the spot within three minutes, and is able to catch the offender. We formed the opinion that our Scotland Yard might profitably study the methods of the Chicago police. After visiting the finger-print department, which seemed very efficiently run, we were taken out in one of the cruising police cars. As we drove, we kept on hearing messages being flashed out to cars from headquarters, giving them instructions as to their movements. We passed through some of the worst slum districts, and were pleased to see that some of the streets were marked down for demolition next spring under the Public Works Administration. I never saw a worse state of dilapidation, squalor, dreariness and general degradation. I should be a gangster myself if I had to live in such a place. But it was encouraging to hear from all the Americans we met that they were ashamed of such places, and realized that they were the real breeding-ground of crime. The real improvement in the situation, however, was manifested firstly by the pleasure with which we were told that this and that bad street was being demolished, and the inhabitants rehoused in other areas, and secondly by the talk of the police commissioner who accompanied us. He showed us first this house, now that, all boarded up and deserted, where two years ago policemen were killed in fights with gangsters, and then a street now apparently quiet and respectable, which was formerly unsafe for outsiders to enter. We felt that things were definitely on the mend in Chicago

We saw the open space where Communist and Socialist speakers address open-air meetings—a safety-valve for the submerged tenth in the Chicago back-streets. One wonders why the Socialist movement has made so little headway in the United States of America. When I visited the headquarters of the American Socialist Party I found as good intellectual leaders as one could find anywhere in Europe. But the Socialist movement in America suffers from two handicaps. Firstly, America was so long a land of individuals, pioneering alone in the backwoods for their own gain, that social restrictions are unpopular. If they are admitted now as a necessity, they are accepted only as practical measures of temporary significance, as palliatives, and not as the result of clear thinking based on a political theory. Secondly, the Socialist movement of America has no foundation in the great trade union organizations which are such a feature of English political life. It remains an intellectual movement without a great industrial organization at its back.

We left Chicago with a feeling of wonder mingled with hopefulness. The city seemed at first sight the most imposing we had yet seen in America. But appearances were deceptive. If one got behind the Michigan Avenue, one had the feeling that Chicago had been, and to some extent still was, a "whited sepulchre." Insulls and Rockefellers had lived on the whited exterior. Inside were the dead men's bones of the slums, the Latin and Slav quarters from which had sprung the poisonous fungus of organized crime. Now Insull's prestige has fallen and Prohibition is ended. But until the authorities clear out the sepulchre and make it a wholesome soil where the human plant can grow to its full stature, they will not be able to congratulate themselves without reserve. No other city in the United States has such a task—to live down and repair the ravages of decades of uncontrolled nineteenth-century individualism.

CHAPTER V

THE MIDDLE WEST

FOR some years past English people have been dimly aware that there was a great body of American opinion away out on the prairies of the Upper Mississippi and across the Appalachians which did not think like the rest of the country. They have pictured the Middle Westerners as backwoods farmers, uninterested in the fate of the world outside, sour, grasping, and relentless, demanding payment of the War Debt to the uttermost farthing, heedless of the warnings of internationally-minded professors at Yale and Harvard, and of public opinion in the East in touch with Europe. As for ourselves, we had been in touch since we landed with feeling in New York, New England and Chicago. We had heard much hostile comment, among business people, men of affairs, students and intellectuals, of the Roosevelt Administration. The criticism was often conflicting, and varied with the type of critic. Moreover, I thought I had found less rigid Conservatism in Chicago than further East. And it seemed to us that the further West we went the more mellow opinion seemed to become. The grasping backwoods farmer was fading into the background by the time we arrived, one morning late in October, at Des Moines, the capital of the State of Iowa. Clearly one could not expect to know anything of America if one did not get in touch with the great agricultural areas lying east of the Rockies and south of the Great Lakes.

Our first impression of Des Moines, on the morning of October 29th, was not exhilarating. There was a grey sky and a cold autumn nip in the air as we left the station and drove through the dull, drab, smoky streets of the business

quarter of the town. Des Moines was long past the pioneer
stage of development which my father noted when he crossed
the continent in 1869. Here and there a weather-beaten
wooden house gave a glimpse of what the town was once like.
But now twenty-storied business blocks and hotels darkened
the main streets, and the factories and motor-car assembly-
plants showed how far industrialism had invaded the city
during the last thirty years. Presently we came to the houses
of the manual and clerical workers—wooden bungalows with
verandas and open spaces round them, much pleasanter
than the rows of brick barracks in which similar people
live in England—and then the villas of the more prosperous
inhabitants. These last were mostly imitations of what
Europe is producing. It seemed that the richer the owner,
the more he wanted his house to imitate Hampton Court
or the stately country seats of England. I admit that imita-
tion is the sincerest flattery, but somehow I felt that these
houses were a little out of place in the Middle West. The
houses of the workers were much more original and in
keeping with their surroundings.

We had proof before long that there was an enlightened
public opinion in the Middle West which realizes the need
of a social conscience. One day in Des Moines we visited
the relief centres where the unemployed were receiving food-
packages. A number of young people, the daughters of
parents in relatively prosperous circumstances, were giving
their services to the Health and Labour Department,
administering relief according to the regulations laid down
by the Iowa State authority. Their services were given
voluntarily. I could see no trace in these relief-centres of
the patronage which is all too common where private charity
is involved. Here one saw the beginnings of a social service
system which we have long had in England, and the need of
which no one now disputes, but which is only now developing

in the United States as a result of the great depression. I was continually questioned about our social service system in England, and I was surprised and touched by the interest felt in the way the old country manages its affairs.

On our second day in Des Moines we made the acquaintance of the Wallace family. One member of this family is the distinguished Secretary for Agriculture in Washington. We met his brother and sister-in-law, and through them came into contact with the farming population. The Wallace family are enterprising and progressive Middle Westerners who have a printing business in Des Moines, started by one of their forebears, a farm in the country, about ten miles to the North, and a plant where maize seed is extracted and collected. Here business is combined with research. It was our privilege to see their farm on our second day in Des Moines. We drove out in a car and got our first impression of the open country of the Middle West. The land is gently undulating, so that the horizon is seldom more than six or eight miles distant. The countryside is dotted with little farms of roughly eighty to a hundred acres each. Twenty to thirty acre fields of corn, alfalfa grass and wheat are separated by barbed wire fences. It being autumn, the maize was stooked in the fields, and the wheat was long since harvested, while hogs and small Hereford store cattle roamed the stubbles. Here and there the half-dried beds of streams showed that this part of Iowa had been near the drought zone, and we heard stories of serious conditions further to the south. But here the countryside looked placid and quietly hopeful. Nature was not bursting with abundance, but she was not too hard a task-master. Indeed, one of the troubles to-day was the bountifulness of Nature and the inability of the people to buy the produce of the farms. It was hard to imagine that two years ago farmers had been unable to sell their corn and hogs, except at prices below the cost of production, and the county sheriff, who had been sent to distrain for taxes, had been tied to a tree with a halter round his neck. On looking at the quiet countryside with its broad fields, brown in the autumn sun, its quiet little streams, its stretches of rough birch and pine woodland, and its little farms, with children playing in the courtyard, as children play all over the world, I thought of the lines of Arthur Gutterman:

> "Still the valleys are rich and green,
> The air is good, the sky is clear,
> The corn still marches in crested ranks,
> The woods still wave on the mountain flanks,
> The squirrel still knows where his nuts are hid,
> The river still flows as it always did,
> The cows still graze in their old content
> In spite of human mismanagement."

We were taken to see the farm of a typical Iowan pioneering family. They were of Middle Western farming stock, Quakers and descendants of the frontiersmen who had come in from the East over half a century ago. One could almost see the stern lines of the Pilgrim Fathers written on their faces. Their spiritual food was Evangelical Christianity, the Bible, a healthy belief that all men are born equal, and hard work. Their material food was potato-soup with Maryland chicken, waffles and pumpkin pie, or at least that was the fare they put before us. As I looked round the room I could almost see the shades of Thomas Jefferson and Abraham Lincoln watching over us. But these descendants of the old pioneers had an outlook wider than that of their forebears. They were anxious to hear about Europe, and above all about England. How were the farmers getting on there? Were conditions any better than with them? Was there any chance of better trade between the nations, which would enable them to sell some of their corn and hogs abroad?

What early pioneer would have thought of such things as the affairs of foreign countries? "Manifest Destiny" would carry Columbia forward, and Europe could look after herself. To-day Europe and Columbia, or at least the Anglo-Saxon nations, must pull together if we are ever to get out of this mess we are in. I could see that the world had narrowed greatly since the days of the Pioneers. I fancy the World War must have done a great deal towards giving the young men of the Middle West a new outlook. Several members of our host's family had been in the war and had seen something of Europe and England. They were beginning to realize that America is part of the greater world.

The ladies of the household also, though reared on the Ten Commandments and the American Constitution, were looking further afield today. Ladies' fashions and Hollywood films were among their requirements, though I did not see a wireless set. My host was anxious to show me all there was to see on the farms. I marvelled at the row of motor-cars belonging to the agricultural labourers in his employ. I have not seen a British agricultural labourer who could manage to own even a motor-bicycle. On the farm I found a much higher standard of dairy herd management than is common in England. Cattle were regularly tested for tuberculosis by State officials. Bull Indexes were being used as a measure for recording milk yields and butter fat, and improving the herds. The average yield of milk and of butter fat content was higher than the average in England. Of course the conditions obtaining on this farm may not have been typical of the poorer and smaller farms, but I was to see some of these later, and I got much the same impression—that the American dairy industry is far ahead of ours. In order to get a better notion of the average Middle Western farmer we were taken to see some small farms of men who worked a hundred acres with a wife and one permanent young man, and seasonal labour in the summer. I will describe one such farm, which was fairly typical. The farmhouse was of wood, single storied with veranda, and surrounded by gaunt elm-trees, standing in an open expanse of country, chequered with corn and alfalfa fields. The sheds also were of wood, and here were housed implements, cattle and hogs, the store cattle roaming the stubble, while those destined for the packing-factory were penned in the buildings for fattening. The wife saw to the poultry, as in England, and they wandered round the buildings and laid their eggs anywhere and everywhere, especially where they were not wanted. The young farmer took me round the place. We talked about farming prospects, and I could have imagined that I was back in England. The words were just the same, but instead of the English countryman's drawl I heard the sharp Yankee accent. Prices were too low, taxation was too high, the Government was not doing enough, and yet had too many officials, and was too expensive for the country. I suppose the countryman's mind is much the same everywhere. Yet he admitted that there had been an improvement under the Roosevelt Administration. He had agreed to reduce his acreage and had not bred so many hogs. It seemed wrong to limit Nature in this way, but prices were considerably higher than last year, and although he had less to sell this year, he had benefited from the processing tax and he thought that a little more money was coming in now. He was thankful to the President and Mr. Wallace and the drought for this help! He would be able to keep his head above water, and perhaps pay his State and Federal taxes this year, which he had not done for two years. On another farm I visited near by I found that the farmer had been in receipt of public relief for six months. He had not been able to feed his family, which was a large one, as his land was one of the poor sub-marginal farms which he had taken up

I   129

years ago. He could manage when prices were good, but when they slumped these farms were the first to suffer, because the yield was too low. Yet he could not move. He and his family were frozen in there by the slump. How was he to get out? Only the State could move him to better lands, and that was obviously what would have to be done, unless he was to stay on public relief indefinitely. I found the system of taxation very different from that of England, and in many ways not so fair. Taxes were assessed on the capital value of a farmhouse and land, and they were payable whether the farm was occupied or not, and whether it was making a profit or not. Also it seemed to me that the burden of rural education was not well distributed, at least in this part of the State. A district that built a school had to pay for it out of local taxes. The burden was not spread over the State, or even over the country, as in England, but had to be borne by a small area with perhaps not more than 1,000 inhabitants, equal to a Rural District area in England. This penalized the progressive areas.

Since the advent of the Roosevelt Administration the Federal Government has been faced with the task of explaining to the public the need for curtailing the production of food at a time when large numbers of people in the industrial centres are not eating enough. One cannot altogether argue this question on first principles. The United States, as it seems to me, has been faced with a very special problem. During the war forty million acres of new land were brought under cultivation to feed Europe. Since then Europe has been doing her best to make it impossible for America to send her produce across the Atlantic. Of course, the United States is partly to blame, as its high tariffs have evoked retaliatory restrictions in Europe. But the Roosevelt Administration has been faced with a situation which was none of its own making. I hardly see how the Government could have handled the situation, obtaining in 1933, except by attempting to organize the planned production of food, thereby bringing it into relation with the existing consumers' demand. Regarded as an emergency measure, and not as a permanent policy, the arguments in favour of such action seem to me unanswerable. It is a temporary remedy, pending the rise in consumers' buying power through the operation of the industrial side of the New Deal. And it has this great advantage, that it forces people who have hitherto never thought that anything else was needed to achieve prosperity but to work hard for oneself, get everything possible out of the land, turn it into money, and pass on to some other State, to organize for the first time in its history. It is now realized that planning on a national scale, in co-operation with one's neighbours, is a sheer necessity, and Uncle Sam is buckling down to his new task with his usual energy.

I found when I visited the State agricultural College of Ames that the staff there were taking the lead in assisting the farmers' committees which had been formed all over the State of Iowa to plan their production for several years ahead. In this respect they have gone further than we have in England, but then we have no surplus of home produce, and have a large import trade which competes with home produce. But here in the United States I found that steps were being taken to plan the production of wheat and maize in the State of Iowa for the year 1935. The farmers' committees arranged among themselves how the acreage should be allotted and by how much each farmer should reduce his head of hogs. Large numbers of surplus hogs and cattle had been sent to supply the soup-kitchens for the unemployed in the towns. These farmers' committees are very like the Farmers' Union Organization in our own country—voluntary associations of farmers which have been recognized by the Government as able to speak for agriculture as a whole, and are being utilized to work out a policy in co-operation with, and not at the dictation of the Government. In this respect we and our American cousins are working along much the same lines. When we must depend on the Governments, we make sure that it is our servant and not our master.

I found that the incidence of the processing tax was being carefully studied at Ames College. They had found that in 1934 a 10 per cent processing tax had produced a 20 per cent rise in hog prices, but that the rise had been borne partly by the consumer and partly by the big packing companies, which had not raised their retail prices for finished products, but had been content with a lower turnover and so with lower net earnings. It seems, therefore, that as far as the products of the Middle West corn and hog belt are concerned, the consumers are not bearing the whole burden of pulling the farmer out of the rut of the depression. The situation has been to some extent complicated by the drought in the States immediately east of the Rockies, so that a certain allowance must be made for wholesale price increases due to this cause. Nevertheless, it cannot be doubted that the schemes of planned production have played a most important rôle in the recovery. The situation had become desperate. In some Middle Western States as much as 10 per cent of farm properties had come into the hands of mortgagees through foreclosure, and tenant farming was rapidly on the increase. This process has been definitely arrested.

I found that, while much progress has been made in the Middle West as regards the planning of farm production, little has been done in the direction of organizing the marketing of produce along the lines of our Agricultural Marketing Act in England. I found in the Eastern States and in New England that a beginning had been made to organize producers into co-operative associations which were recognized by the Federal Government, and were given power to fix wholesale prices. This system was in practice only in the dairy industry, and was not working any too well there. By the licensing of distributors the Dairy Produce Section of the Agricultural Adjustment Administration in Washington, which corresponds in some ways with our Milk Marketing Board, but with nothing like the powers of the latter, was trying to control milk prices. But there was no machinery for the defence of consumers' interests, and no means of inquiry into distributors' costs. This last difficulty is unsolved in England also, but at least we in England have a watertight organization of milk producers which fixes wholesale prices by negotiations. But the great obstacle to anything of this kind in America is the Constitution of the United States. There is an ever-present fear in the minds of politicians, statesmen, economists, and all who aim at the better marketing of produce, that the large private corporation or the small speculator and price-cutter will block the way to reform, by an appeal to the Supreme Court and the Constitution. I have a feeling that the United States has still to get out of the shell in which uncontrolled individualism and State rights have encased it. Many first-class issues affecting inter-State trading are pending before the Supreme Court at the present time.[1] As matters stand now a Federal Board has only power to regulate the prices of milk or other products passing from State to State, but has no power to regulate that part of the products which is sold within the State. Of course, modern methods of price regulation and agreement become impossible under such conditions. Any small price-cutter can upset an agreement and appeal to the Constitution. I found

[1] This was written before the famous decision of the Supreme Court in June 1935, which largely bore out these remarks.

that in Iowa there was a local agreement in respect of all the milk produced and sold locally. But there was no arrangement in respect of anything sold outside the State. I heard that there was only one State—namely, Rhode Island—where satisfactory agreements had been reached concerning the prices of State-produced and inter-State milk.

On the other hand, I found that the power of the Packing Companies, of which I had seen the central depôts in Chicago, was very great, and becoming even greater. They are handling an increasing quantity of farm products in the Middle West, and are not confining their activities to meat and meat products. Their collecting depôts for livestock, dairy and poultry products are to be seen at all important centres along the railway lines and main roads from Chicago to the Rockies. These corporations may not openly oppose marketing schemes and controlled prices, as the small distributors and producers do, but they use these schemes to establish their domination over the market, and resist any attempt to inquire into distributing costs. In England too our farmers are up against the bacon curers and the big dairy companies in the cities, and we are a long way from achieving a satisfactory solution. But these problems have hardly yet been faced in the United States.

In this connection I inquired after my return from Ames College into the various independant political movements among farmers in the Middle West. I found in Des Moines a body called the Farmers' Union. It was a militant body of people who professed either to be farmers or to have been farmers. Their leaders seemed to be journalists and professional men, the chief being Milo Reno, whom I did not see, as he was away. This movement arose in the hectic days of the price collapse, before the Roosevelt Government came into power and effectively resisted foreclosures and the sale of produce at ruinous prices. I had the impression that the New Deal, and the awakening of the Democratic Party to the need of an agricultural programme, had largely taken the wind out of the sails of the Farmers' Union. Their leaders, when I interviewed them, could only justify their existence by picking out little points in the Agricultural Adjustment Programme, magnifying them, and trying to work themselves up into a state of indignation. At times I even detected a reactionary note, as when I was told that schemes for controlling the price of farm produce interfered with the sacred rights of the States! There seemed to be a good deal of confused thinking among the members of this militant organization, and possibly there was a lack of disinterested leadership. I did not gather that it was widely supported now, although it undoubtedly played a big part and did much good in the early stage of the collapse. There are other and more successful independent farmers' movements further north, where the fertile plains of the Upper Mississippi merge into the poorer, stony, undulating lands of Minnesota and Wisconsin. This region is a dairy land with surplus milk which has to be made into cheese and butter. The "rugged individualism" of the farmers of these parts seems to have been directed into a collectivist channel. They have realized sooner than other farmers in the Middle West that their particular problem of handling surplus milk can be solved only by co-operative effort. Leaders of strong personality have arisen among them, and have given their movement a political colour; indeed, many of the remedies proposed are frankly Socialist in all but name. For several years the Farmers' Party has ruled Minnesota, with the vigorous Governor Olsen at its head. They demand the nationalization of transport, banking, and the packing corporations. The La Follette brothers at the head of an independent party in the neighbouring State of Wisconsin, are hardly less advanced. Still, I do not anticipate the rise of a third or Agrarian Party in the United States. Independent movements have been common in the past. A century ago the election of Thomas Jefferson as President was a revolt of the backwoods farmer against the aristocratic East. The Free Silver movement and the William Bryan agitation was the demand of the Western farmers for liberation from the financial strangle-hold of New York and Chicago. The Theodore Roosevelt's "Bull Moose" Party of thirty years ago aimed at the Trusts. But in most cases compromises were made with one of the two great parties of the Federal Congress. It seems that the same thing is happening again. The history of the Middle West is the history of a struggle between the debtor West and the creditor East.

On the last evening of our stay at Des Moines there was a Grand Rally of the Democratic Party held before the election, which was to take place in a week's time. For an Englishman it was a little bit puzzling to understand just what was happening at this election. It seemed that people were being elected for every conceivable post, from that of Governor to that of the office boy who licks the stamps at the local Registrar's office. The campaign appeared to be progressing very peaceably. There was none of the noise and bluster which one had always heard were inseparable from American elections. The electors gave one the impression of soberly considering the issues. There was much distribution of literature and posters in streets, but I did not see any house-to-house canvassing, as one does in an English election. Meetings were held in the evening, at halls or public rooms; and I saw no open-air assemblies. In general I had the impression that the fight was mainly journalistic and literary. The spoken word was the second line of attack. But the most powerful influence in securing votes was neither the press nor the platform, but just the prospects

136

of a job if your party got in and the prospect of getting the sack if your party got beaten.

We went to see the Grand Democratic Rally. A prominent citizen of Des Moines escorted us. He was typical of the cultured and travelled American. He took us to the offices of a local newspaper, where we could see the Democratic procession go by, headed by a donkey, the symbol of the Party, and numerous placards, some poking good-humoured fun at the Republicans. A bedraggled effigy of an elephant was paraded, under which was written—"Good-bye, G.O.P.: we shall not be seeing you!" On other placards were words exhorting the electors to vote for this man and that. I saw one which bore the words: "Vote for Judge of the County Court." On seeing this I innocently remarked: "Funny to elect judges." "Funny!" said my American companion; "it isn't funny, it's a tragedy!" And he went on to dilate upon the evil effects of the spoils system; how in one city, when a new mayor was elected, he put his epileptic nephew in as manager of the urban gas-works! 'How can we expect a capable civil service or a judicial system which is above reproach if we make them the game of party politics?" It certainly seems to me that the English system of keeping the judicial, administrative and legislative systems separate, and yet linked together by invisible, silken cords, is the best, provided one can get just that fine adjustment which enables the three component systems to balance. But at least there is this to be said for the American system: it does allow the man in the street to have a say in everything that goes on in the country. If only one could retain that principle, without making every clerk in the municipal offices tremble for his living every time there is an election, a great advance would be made.

After the Democratic Procession there was a grand meeting in a public hall. My wife and I, as guests, were given seats on the platform. The hall was gaily decked with the Stars and Stripes, and was crowded. One soon got an idea of the curious way in which national or Federal and local politics are intermingled at elections in the United States. At this election the voter had to vote for a long list of persons, from the Congressman who represented him in national affairs to the auditor of the accounts of the local lunatic asylum! This is a complete contrast to England, where the election of local District Councillors and County Councillors is quite unconnected with the election of members of the Imperial Parliament. It leads, in America, to a curious mingling of local and national issues. For instance, the proceedings at this meeting were opened by all the candidates, both for local office and for the Federal Congress, marching on to the platform, and rising in batches, and being cheered by the meeting! Fortunately they did not all make speeches, or we should have been there all night. But a certain number were put up to speak, and they all gave short reports on what they had done while they were in office. This phase of the meeting was concluded by the retiring Governor of the State, who spoke for half an hour, and gave a detailed account of his administrative work during his term of office. This was the sort of thing one might have heard in England at a municipal election in November, when the mayor would describe how he handled the local unemployment relief, or report on the state of the local water supply. This was followed by a speech from the candidate for the Lower House of Congress, who began at once to talk about the New Deal, the Labour Codes, the questions of tariffs and foreign trade, and the banking situation; in other words, national and international politics, which we should hear discussed only at a Parliamentary general or by-election. Thus in America one finds a curious mixture of issues. But the advantage of the system seems to be that any issue can

be raised. Like the American Constitution, it is very democratic in theory, but in practice it tends to be confusing.
The English system leads to a concentration of public
opinion on one or two main issues at either national or local
elections. And so we saw in Des Moines how we and the
Americans, with our equally democratic systems, have
nevertheless developed them along different lines in the
course of the century and a half that have elapsed since our
political separation.

CHAPTER VI

ACROSS PRAIRIE AND PLATEAU

A TRAVELLER on a journey across this continent soon realizes that not only are there forty-eight States in the Union, but that the United States is really not a country at all, but a continent in which there are at least six physical divisions with quite separate climates and systems of economy. Moreover, the peoples living in these six areas have each their special mentality and outlook on life. Though all are Americans, their surroundings and their mode of livelihood give them an individual way of thinking and acting. We had seen in the East and New England an industrial and manufacturing population culturally in touch with Europe, protectionist by tradition but becoming deeply concerned for its industrial future. In the Middle West we had seen the great agricultural lands, populated by farmers who were worrying about surplus produce and unsaleable crops. Further to the West, in the Rocky Mountains and their foothills, we were to see the dry plateau, the land of grazing ranches, where in the past the pioneer whites had wrested the soil from the buffaloes and the Indians, and where they were now in danger of being overwhelmed by drought and the results of unrestricted private exploitation. These comprise three of the great physical and economic divisions of the North American continent. We had seen two of them, and in the course of the next few days we were to see the third. We entered the Transcontinental train on the Rock Island Railway which left Des Moines for the West on the morning of November 1st.

For all the rest of the day, and all the following night, the train rolled slowly westwards. It was not a fast Transcontinental express, but very comfortable, with good beds, lounge, and dining-room. We stopped frequently at little wayside stations in Nebraska, where we got out and walked about. Next morning I rose early to see the sunrise on the prairies. We were now in the naturally dry country, which resembles the Russian steppe. Dry conditions are more or less normal here, though human agencies have been at work for many years which are reducing the value of these lands to the danger-point for human subsistence. One could now look across great sweeps of country for fifteen or twenty miles whenever the train passed over a slight elevation. Prairie and even desert grass grew in tufts that became uprooted and blew for miles like balls in the wind. A few cattle were grazing, and here and there was a ranching station in which could be seen not buck-jumping ponies and rodeo riders with Mexican hats and saddles, as the Hollywood films show them, but rusty old motor-cars, petrol-tins and junk! Thus has the twentieth century altered the Western prairies. Indeed, it is possible that modern agriculture may eliminate the whole ranching industry process, by concentrated rearing and feeding methods. On these ranches is now raised the young stock which is sent eastwards to be fattened in stalls or on better pastures. The whole process might be simplified by rearing and fattening the stock in the same locality. Hitherto the great advantage of the ranching process has been its cheapness, but with the spread of dry conditions on the prairies and over-grazing its productive capacity has been falling, and meanwhile newer methods are tending to cheapen the rearing of young stock on farms in the old settlements further East. This may lead in time to the conversion of the Western prairies into game ranches and pleasure parks, while the former prairie population will be shifted back East again to subsistence farms. What a fine playground the Western prairies might become for the recreation of the Eastern city-dwellers! We might also see buffalo herds once more roaming wide tracts of national reserves. A change indeed from the late nineteenth century! Apparently a trek backwards, but not in reality. The United States will only be planning, for the first time in its history, to profit by its great Western heritage.

On the morning of November 1st the train rolled into Colorado Springs, and we saw the Rocky Mountains a little to the west.

Here we hired a car, and drove some distance along the foothills. We could see in the east the prairies falling gradually towards the basin of the Mississippi and its twin brother, the Missouri. We passed small ranching stations— ugly collections of flat-roofed mud houses, with a store, a cattle and sheep pen, a water-tower, and the usual dumps for old motor-cars. The settlers here were evidently having a bad time of it. Caught in two dry seasons with over-stocked land, they had suffered from soil erosion, and from the dry winds that have scoured the great plains for the last two summers. I gathered that some families here were in receipt of public relief, as many of their cattle had died. This land had been overstocked, and the herbage was deteriorating, so that the surface soil was being blown away by the winds. Relief works had been started by the Federal authority, and some of the settlers were working on forest preservation schemes in the mountains in a Civil Conservation Camp. Think of the descendants of Buffalo Bill in receipt of public relief and working in Federal camps, while the remnants of the Indians dress and dance for tourists! A new America is indeed arising—but probably a better America than the old, if only one could see to the end of the process.

The truth is that a surplus and unwanted population in recent years has come into existence on these prairies. The Department of Agriculture in Washington is aware of this, and, as far as the States, with their jealousy of Washington, will allow, it is beginning to find new occupations for these stranded people, by organizing public works and the preservation of national resources. Yet it is thought that some proportion of the population will have to emigrate, for extensive subsistence farming can hardly be possible on these arid plains. Sixty years ago my father crossed this country and found that all here was hope and activity, the emigrants pouring West and the railways being built to carry them, while the enterprising worker was rewarded with wealth and power. Now one finds unemployment, poverty, dying cattle, railway companies unable to pay dividends, and settlers drifting East, or working on Federal relief!

The next stage of our journey was covered in the Denver, Rio Grande and Western daily train, which passes up the Royal Gorge of the Rocky Mountains. The railway ran in a southerly direction to Pueblo, and then struck off to the west, rising steadily for some miles through a steep gorge. Presently the gorge broadened out into open plateaux and upland valleys, the lofty mountain peaks rising on either hand. These were covered with snow. The inhabitants of these mountain valleys lived by a mixture of mining, ranching and forest work. We passed big lead mines from time to time, and large mining settlements, where the train stopped, indicating that there was still a fairly busy population there in spite of the depression. I gathered that the copper ore mined here was of low grade, but that the high American tariff enables the industry to compete with the Rhodesian ores. Otherwise these mining valleys would be derelict. The little towns or large villages of the mining district were composed of wooden buildings, but I missed the planless disorder and the devil-may-care atmosphere which one associates with American mining settlements. From the types that I saw at the stations I should set the miners down as law-abiding people. Large stone-built stores or shops, churches, and cinemas were in evidence in most places. In the open country there were small ranches, mainly for sheep, and here and there a lumber camp for the provision of timber for local needs. After dark we settled down in the parlour car. Quite apart from the comfort and efficiency of railway travel in America, one is struck by the congenial company nearly always to be found on board. At the same time one must avoid the error of thinking that all one hears from fellow-passengers in the parlour car of a transcontinental train is representative of American opinion. It is generally representative of a certain type of opinion, the opinion of business and professional men, who are the most frequent travellers. These, I found, were mainly hostile to the New Deal, and to the President, and were still inclined to think in terms of the pre-slump period. After conversing with a company of American business men in a parlour car I always felt that I should like to talk with the lone horseman watching his flock of sheep and looking up at the train as it passed by, and hear what he thought of the President and the New Deal. Nevertheless, it is wonderful to note how optimistic the Americans are in the midst of their troubles and difficulties. This quality of optimism seems to be common to all classes. They are always smiling and jolly; and their speech, moreover, is refreshingly vivid. It seems redolent of the air of the prairies. My mind always seemed like a dusty attic compared to theirs—at least, as regards the power of expression. Such a nation will never be down and out. The Americans are at last interested in other nations, and ready to learn from those which are older in experience. But there is no sign of what I noticed in Russia even in the midst of the great upheaval—namely, a self-critical attitude. Here, I felt, there was self-assurance tempered with readiness to learn. There was also the greatest and most genuine friendliness towards English people, and a flattering desire to prove some family connection with former English settlers in America. I cannot understand how the Hearst newspapers get their readers. One sees very little of these papers in public places. The only time I was conscious of the Hearst atmosphere was when I was talking to a municipal officer and the chief of police in a certain city. They were Irish. And there, I think, is the cue which explains what anti-British feeling may still linger in the United States. Tammany is not only corrupt, but the source of a certain amount of discord between the two English-speaking peoples.

Next morning (November 3rd) I rose early again. The train had descended from the steep valleys of the Rockies, and we were rolling along north-westwards, over a high plateau about 4,000 feet above sea-level. The land was becoming half prairie again. High ranges of mountains lay to the east and west of us. We had entered the Great Salt Lake plateau in the State of Utah. The villages and settlements that we passed were now all agricultural. Wheat, maize, alfalfa were grown, and, where the land could be irrigated, apples and plums. Here were the first Mormon settlements, but there was nothing distinctive about them. They might have been the settlements of any white Americans. My father noted that the Mormons were almost the only settlers on this plateau in 1869, and commented on the tidy and industrious appearance of their settlements. They still look tidy and industrious, but they are not now distinctively Mormon. In the last fifty years people of all races and religious persuasions have come into this valley. The Mormons have been to a large extent absorbed into the great melting-pot.

About eight o'clock our train pulled into Salt Lake City, the famous capital of the Mormons. Sixty-six years ago my father came here to interview Brigham Young. I wondered, as we arrived in the city, if I should find many changes since those days. The Mormon question was then a very acute one. The Puritan New Englanders were agitating to clear out the nest of dissolute fanatics, as they thought the Mormons, and drive them from their mountain fastnesses. Fortunately wiser counsels prevailed, and the question was left to solve itself. Polygamy was the result of a surplus of women in a land where mortality among the men was apt to be heavy, and where there was great need for a pioneer people to increase their numbers. It was the passing of the early pioneer phase, quite as much as pressure from Washington, that led to the extinction of polygamy.

Having fixed our headquarters at the large hotel run by the Mormon Church we spent the day going round the city.

Next to Washington, it was the best laid-out city that we had seen in the United States. In the city itself the long wide streets were planted with poplar. The houses were mainly of stone and brick, and strict building regulations have ensured plenty of open spaces. There were no slums. In the working-class quarters round the railway centre some of the houses were of wood, but there was no overcrowding, and the general conditions seemed good.

We drove outside the city into the open plateau. At the edge of the mountain range, about five miles from the city, we saw the spot where Brigham Young with his first pioneers came down from the mountains, entered the plains, and decided to found the first settlement. Here was a monument, and a fine view was obtained across the Salt Lake plains. Although it was a dull day the outlook was pleasing. Around us was the stony desert and the rough ground of the foothills of the Rockies all white with the late autumn snow. Large flocks of sheep were being brought down from the mountains to their winter quarters on the plains by Mormon shepherds on horses. The stony wilderness was quick with life. Later in the day I walked some six or seven miles into the cultivated corn lands and orchards, where irrigation had made the desert blossom like the rose. How all this reminded me of Central Asia, and how similar human life is over wide areas of the Earth when Nature sets bounds to man's activity! Yet culture and religion are not without their influence. In Turkestan mosques, minarets and bazaars speak of the great cult of Islam. Here the golden archangel on the Mormon Temple and the advertisements for Standard Oil and toothpastes indicate the conquest of the Salt Lake plateau by Anglo-Saxon Protestant commercialism from the East.

We went to the Capitol, a fine, dome-shaped building, the seat of the Government of the State of Utah. This capitol was built shortly before the World War, and the whole of the money was found by the State within two years of its erection. Mormon thrift is proverbial. But of course the Mormons are not the sole religious community in the State. They make up only 40 per cent of the population of Salt Lake City, but they still very largely give the tone to the place. The museum in the Capitol contains some objects of art and a very fine marble hall. But the decorations in the State Reception Room reminded us of the house of an upstart millionaire. The people who showed us round seemed to think it much more important that a curtain should contain ten thousand dollars' worth of gold thread than that the colour of the curtain should blend with the colour of the rest of the room. I received the impression that taste has still to be acquired in Salt Lake City. Yet here again everybody was amazingly friendly. As soon as they heard that we had come from England, their faces beamed, and they began to tell us long stories of their forebears who came from England. In fact, I could see that England was still in a sense

147

their old home, although they had been good American citizens for at least one or two generations. I kept on meeting all day persons who told us that their fathers or grandfathers came from England because they heard of Joseph Smith's preaching, and were inspired to leave their home, brave the hardships of the great caravan trek across the continent in the face of hostile Indians, and join the gallant band of Mormon pioneers.

The whole thing is an amazing story. Joseph Smith and Brigham Young really believed that they were gathering the lost tribe of Israel to a desolate spot where they would escape the Doom of the Last Judgment when the wrath of God should destroy all the world but the chosen Latter Day Saints. Having braved the Indians and got to the Salt Lake plains they waited, but the Last Trumpet did not sound. So there was nothing for the disillusioned saints to do but to settle down and make corn grow where desert grass grew before. And this they did with characteristic Mormon efficiency. About one hundred years ago it was fairly common for this kind of movement to get going, especially in New England, settled as it was by people descended from the more fanatical of the Dutch and English Puritans. Darwin had not yet arisen to make hay of ideas of this sort, and the thought of trekking into the desert to wait, as the chosen tribe for the Last Judgment, was really rationalizing their religion. Trekking West to land that cried for settlers was a natural and proper urge. This curious religious idea was doubtless the cement that bound these people together in the face of hostile Indians, cold and hunger.

We had a taste of the Mormon atmosphere when we went to the Tabernacle—an enormous dome unsupported by pillars—to hear the great organ play. A recital is given every day at noon. The organ used to be the largest in the world. On this day the organist played the Prelude to *Lohengrin*, and played it excellently. But the most interesting part of the programme was a Mormon hymn of which we were given the words. According to this part the Mormon creed seemed to embrace the transmigration of souls, and the belief that man is not born sinful, but rises to higher spheres according to the life he leads on earth.

Before we left Salt Lake City we became a centre of interest for newspaper reporters, and we had to pose for the camera and give an interview. I was struck by the fact that the reporters did not ask me, as they always used to do in America, what I thought of their country and people. Instead of this they asked me to tell them how England was dealing with industrial depression, and what were the prospects of the British Labour Party at the next election. Mormonism and religious controversy too were things of the past. The people of Salt Lake City and Utah are thinking of the society of the future in this world, rather than of the Last Trumpet which will usher in the next. Going about the town I found the place full of electioneering placards, for the election was to take place in three days' time. Republicans and Democrats were mutually denouncing each other in respect of such mundane affairs as the repairs to the city drains, the soldiers' War Bonus, unemployment relief, the proceeds of the sales tax, and the salary of the Accountant-General. In the Salt Lake City that I saw Roosevelt's New Deal was the issue of the day. In my father's day the issue was the number of Brigham Young's wives. The spirit of Joseph Smith can rest in peace. His people are moving on to new, if mundane, spheres of activity.

On November 4th we took train to Ogden, where we joined the Southern Pacific Line, and caught the fast Transcontinental express. We were soon at the edge of the Great Salt Lake, which is the centre of this high plateau, lying between the Rocky Mountains and the Sierra Nevada on

149

the Pacific coast. In the course of many thousands of years the climate of this plateau has become drier, and water no longer drains into the Pacific, but flows into a great inland lake and there evaporates. Consequently the lake is very saline. The railway crosses the lake by a huge dam for about fifteen miles, and then by a viaduct supported on piles. It also takes advantage of a large tongue of land for about ten miles. It was a weird sight as the train rode cautiously over the limpid waters on great wooden piles. Along the edge of the lake were barren salt pans and mud flats. There was no living thing in the water, neither fish nor bird, save a tiny crayfish which continues to live there. We looked out across the salt watery waste and saw towards the horizon great mirages of mountain ranges. The spirit of the Great Unknown seemed to brood over the place. On one of the islands, within sight, was a herd of wild buffalo, put there to live out their days in freedom. For no man ever comes this way except to cross it on the narrow thread of steel that binds the Atlantic to the Pacific.

After crossing the Lake we continued over some eighty miles of howling wilderness. This was the Great American Desert, consisting of great salt-pans and saline flats, with occasional thickets of the few plants that can stand such conditions. I pitied the poor railwaymen who had to live and work along this section of the line. Later on the soil improved slightly. We were ascending towards the next range of mountains, the Sierra Nevada. Signs of desert grass appeared, and here and there springs of sweet water, where Hereford steers could be seen grazing. Soon a few isolated ranches and signs of habitation appeared, and, wonderful to relate, men, not riding in motor-cars, but on that now antiquated animal, the horse. Moreover, the men really did look like rough-riders of the Wild West, with black hats and cowboy trousers. At a wayside station I saw some Indian squaws, rather dirty and degenerate. Then some fine ranches appeared on better grazing land. Large platforms were built beside the railway track to facilitate the driving of cattle on to the trucks for shipping East. Large herds of Hereford cattle now dotted what was a great upland prairie, for the moisture of the Pacific coast was already slightly perceptible. At a fair-sized ranching town the train stopped for some time, and I got out to see what I could. I found placards up announcing that "hobos" in search of work would not get unemployment relief from the local authority, if they came from outside the State of Nevada, but that the Federal Government had a bureau in the town which would look after them. A human touch is slowly pervading American public affairs. Who would have thought of relieving hobos four or even three years ago? Who would have thought that the Wild West would worry about the unemployed? But there was a proof of it, even in the State of Nevada which has a population of 100,000 and is two-thirds the size of Germany. However, life is still pretty rough in these parts, and a revolver may even now settle a dispute in the remoter parts of the State.

All that night we descended through the valleys of the Sierra Nevada, and in the morning found ourselves on the plains of Sacramento. From six thousand feet we had gone down to sea-level, to the detriment of our ears and our general fitness. We had left the dry plateaux and were now in steamy sub-tropical heat. We reached Oakland and crossed the lovely blue bay of San Francisco by ferry. We were in the heart of California. We had reached the Pacific at last.

CHAPTER VII

CALIFORNIA AND THE PACIFIC COAST

OUR first sight of San Francisco was the view as we approached from the water. I was reminded a little of Constantinople. There were white houses and deep blue waters, though sky-scrapers took the place of minarets, and the Golden Gate of the Golden Horn. But the atmosphere was not so clear, for San Francisco is covered for part of the day with either a light mist or a thick summer haze. This is due to the fact that the dry hot plains of Sacramento lie between the snowy Sierra Nevada on the one hand and the Pacific Ocean, with its cold Arctic current running down the coast, on the other. The hot air from the plains flows outward towards the cold current of the ocean and condenses into mist which keeps the city cool on summer days.

On our first day (November 7th) we went out to see something of the city. As usual, we found everything beautifully arranged for the tourist to see. I think there is no country where scientific sight-seeing is better organized than in the United States. San Francisco gave us the impression of being a queer mixture of modern business houses and sky-scrapers from industrial North America and residential houses and small villas of the Spanish colonial type. One can see at once that here the Anglo-Saxon and the Latin civilizations have met. But the Anglo-Saxon element predominates in the people. North American push and energy are evident everywhere. The Latin influence is mainly architectural, and has been adapted by the Northerners. We went to see the Dolores Mission, the first Spanish missionary chapel of the eighteenth century. The friars came here from Mexico, the advance-guard of the

Spanish influence, which crept slowly up the coast from the South. There was a quaint old Catholic church with a modern campanile and a nice walled garden which the monks kept in order. Here I found all sorts of sub-tropical flowers and plants. Some shrubs flower here all the year round and humming-birds can be seen darting from bloom to bloom. It was almost unthinkable that a few days ago we were in deep snow on the Rocky Mountain passes. Coming to the coast we saw where San Francisco's millionaires and business people live in the sub-tropical luxury of walled Spanish villas looking out on the blue but often hazy Pacific. The water is so cold on this coast that there is little sea-bathing. Here we saw the well-known rock where brown seals can be seen basking in the sun. Judging by the photograph which my father took when he was here in 1869, there are far fewer seals on the rock now than then. Wild Nature has been retreating before the advance of Man. We then motored back into the city by the Golden Gate, that narrow stretch of water which divides the Pacific from the wide Bay of San Francisco. There is a scheme to build a great bridge across the water, to connect the city with the north shore of the bay, and then with the east shore at Oakland. It will take some years to carry out, but is part of the Federal development projects, and will be one of the biggest engineering feats of its kind in the world. Away out in the Golden Gate we could see the Federal Penitentiary, situated on a rocky island. Here those who have offended against Federal law are interned for various terms. Incidentally, the notorious Al Capone is there. It was necessary that he should commit an offence against the Federal Government before he could be caught and convicted. He was unwise enough to evade payment of his Federal income-tax. If he had confined himself to his gangster crimes he would probably be free today, for he knew how to bribe or terrorize the State in which he happened to be residing. But Uncle Sam cannot be so easily bribed or terrorized, and this fact is the greatest guarantee of progress in the United States.

Passing along the Golden Gate, even the civilian eye could see that the United States of America has her best guns and forces ranged along this coast, looking towards the Far East. On this coast one felt that one was on the edge of an ocean round whose shores great political and racial issues were ripening for solution.

That evening we had a remarkable illustration of one of the problems which interest California. We visited China-town after dark. Here live 20,000 Chinese. They must be the descendants of the Chinese whom my father saw in 1869, building the railways and doing the unskilled labour of California. Now they are settled in this large quarter of San Francisco, many of them fully naturalized American citizens. A large number, it seems, are engaged in business of every kind, wholesale and retail, but some are still unskilled labourers, working mostly in the great docks which line the bay. The well-to-do Chinese business man is also in much evidence.

In one of the main streets of Chinatown we saw the Republican Committee Rooms for the election just pending. This section of the Chinese population was clearly opposed to the New Deal. But the night we were there saw Chinatown all agog over quite another matter. The streets were full. Chinese drum and fife bands were passing along in endless procession, while troops of school-children and young men's clubs had turned out to welcome General Chai Ting Chai, the hero of the Shanghai resistance to the Japanese, who was on a visit to America. He received a royal welcome as his motor-car, in which sat certain American civic dignitaries, passed along the streets. Everywhere Chinese and American flags were seen flying side by side. It was clear that in this part of the United States the people are keenly interested in the Far East, and that their sympathies are with the Chinese. Elsewhere we saw Chinese newspapers on sale which contained anti-Japanese propaganda. The younger generation of the New China are worshipping at the shrine of Nationalism. In a side street we saw relics of the old China, a Buddhist and a Taoist temple. Here the century-old cults, with their images and gaudy trappings, were still being practised. An old Chinese custodian, who looked as if he had walked out of the Willow Pattern, showed us round one of the temples. I was not surprised to hear that attendance had fallen off.

We saw a Chinese Christian church, I think Presbyterian. Some of the younger people attend the churches; the bulk of them, however, seem to go nowhere, but just profess the religion of Nationalism! A very few worship at the shrine of a new social order. I gathered that there were a few Chinese who were supporting Upton Sinclair in his campaign to "End Poverty in California."

All along the water's edge live the unskilled and dock labourers. They are of every nationality, Chinese, Spanish, negro and white American. Here is the submerged tenth which is of no special nationality. It is they who are beginning to get together to consider ways of improving their condition, but co-operation is not easy to effect between all those different nationalities. White American labour is not yet co-operating whole-heartedly with the unskilled labour of the coloured races in trade unions and industrial councils. On the other hand, it is these people who seem to have given Upton Sinclair his very substantial support. At all events, one thing is clear: San Francisco is very different from what it was in my father's day. Firstly, the members of the Chinese colony have settled down to become good

Americans; secondly, the consciousness of the social question is dividing the Chinese into two political camps, side by side with the white Americans. Thirdly, in the sphere of Far Eastern politics the white and coloured races of California are united in wanting to see a strong and independent China.

Our next trip was across the bay of San Francisco to the East shore, where the cities of Oakland and Berkeley are situated. Here we came to the lovely and leafy gardens of the University Campus, with their palm-trees and tropical flowering shrubs, where strange and brightly coloured birds dart across the open spaces. Here bright and intelligent-faced young American men and women were hastening from one building to another, to attend lectures or to work in the laboratories. We were impressed here, as at all the other universities and colleges that we visited in the United States, by the earnestness and intelligence of the younger generation. This impression was confirmed by our personal contact with a number of young people later.

We spent an evening with a research-worker and his family in the agricultural department. They lived in a small villa, perched on the high ground overlooking the bay towards the Golden Gate. The sun had set and the lights of Berkeley and Oakland formed a brilliant mosaic at our feet, while in the distance the lights of San Francisco twinkled in the evening haze rolling in from the Pacific. The sky was deep blue, shading into pale green where the sun had set. The stars were shining and the waters of the bay were purple. We looked down on the darkening forms of the palm-trees in the tropical gardens, and the evening song of the birds rose up to us. Is it surprising that people who come to live in California never want to leave it? I should think that even the hobos and the unemployed would prefer to live where you can sleep out under the open heavens nearly all the year round and where the air is soft like velvet but invigorating like champagne. Our host for that evening had a young student of the University living with him and his family. The student did the washing up after meals and helped to clean the house. In return he received his board and lodging. Coming from a humble home, this was the only way in which he could obtain his University education. And this is what happens in the case of thousands of students. They work in the hours when they are not studying, and no employment is beneath their dignity.

California is a land of extremes—in climate and also, perhaps consequently, in politics. The atmosphere stimulates an explosive activity in the people. The cool breeze of the Pacific is a preventive of mental sloth. Not many weeks before we arrived the whole of the San Francisco port workers struck for better conditions. Then the seasonal workers on the fruit plantations struck, at the height of the picking season, for better pay, and got it. In response to Upton Sinclair's campaign in the autumn of 1934, committees in pursuance of his "End Poverty in California" programme were formed all over the State, from San Francisco to Los Angeles. On the other hand, the solid forces of Conservatism were massed behind Governor Merriam. There had never been such a line-up of Conservative Republicans and Democrats into one camp before. Does this mean that the Marxian class war, as interpreted by Lenin and Stalin, is breaking out in California? I doubt it. The population of California is too heterogeneous, as regards both race and occupation, for a common objective to be easily found. But California is the home of hot-house growths. Every kind of fruit is produced here on a commercial basis, from apples on the plains of Sacramento to figs and dates in the Valley of Death, which is below sea-level in the Sierra Nevada. In the same way the country breeds extremes of politics, massed reaction on the one hand and Utopian Socialism on the other. All sorts of weird movements are going on in the towns and villages along this coast. Apart from the Sinclair movement there are the "Utopians," a queer mixture of religious revivalism and the charlatanism of a secret society. It seems to be the result of Anglo-Saxon evangelism from New England transplanted in the hot-house atmosphere of California.

The results of the November elections of 1934 in California were surprising and in some respects made history. The defeat of Sinclair was a foregone conclusion. But the size of his minority was surprising, and its distribution even more so. Not only did Sinclair poll a good third of the electors of California but these voters were not confined to San Francisco, Los Angeles, and the large cities. They were scattered fairly evenly throughout the great fruit and farming areas of the plains. Evidently not only the white and coloured unskilled and dock labour of San Francisco and the artisans of the film studios in Los Angeles supported Sinclair, but also the Spanish and Mexican seasonal workers on the plantations. But it was as well that Sinclair was defeated, because he could never have put his programme into operation in the teeth of the rest of the United States and chaos would have ensued if he had tried to carry it out. But his great feat was to have given the respectable and well-to-do people of California the shock of their lives, and to have shown them that do-nothing conservatism rouses opposition in every walk of life. One thing struck us greatly during this Californian election: it was extraordinarily orderly. Nowhere did we see any manifestations of undue excitement. Life went on quite normally. There were no processions, like those we saw in the Middle West. The campaign seemed to be conducted from door to door by the distribution of leaflets and literature and by broadcasting. Americans seem to excel in this kind of propaganda. Excitement there was, of course, but it was confined to discussions between groups of people in their homes and in public places.

We spent the afternoon of November 5th in visiting the Giannini Institute of Agricultural Economics in the University of California at Berkeley. I had letters to the Dean and to other heads of the University. We found that the Institute had been raided by Washington and denuded of a large part of its staff and research-workers. Secretary Wallace and the Federal Administration, struggling with the titanic task of administering the Agricultural Adjustment Act, wanted all the best men that the States could supply. Finally, the Dean said, he had to put his foot down, and say that California could send no more. I think this speaks volumes. The Federal Government is gradually increasing its prestige in the land. No longer are the best brains concentrated in the local centres. The United States is forced under modern conditions to centralize its talents.

Agriculture is the chief industry of the State, and fruit-growing the principal department of agriculture. The collapse in prices and the loss of export markets since 1930 had hit the growers disastrously. The high tariffs which the Republicans put on foreign imports into the United States had caused the rest of the world to cease buying Californian fruit. Even Great Britain's tariff on American fruit had affected Californian exports, but the fall in the value of the dollar had to some extent counteracted the influence of the duty. What could be done to untie the Gordian knot? While discussing this problem with Californians whom I met, I thought of the farmers in my home country in England, who are clamouring for the exclusion of all American apples, insisting that England should supply her own wants.

And then I thought of the English luxury industries which normally send goods to the United States in spite of the tariffs. If American growers can't sell their fruit to us, they won't buy our fine woollens or our gramophones. There is the problem in a nutshell. Somehow the two countries have got to plan a mutual exchange of trade.

How different is the state of affairs in California today from that described in my father's letters, written in 1869! He was here just after the Gold Rush to these Western valleys, when the virgin land was still largely unoccupied, the main trouble being the absence of suitable settlers and the cornering of good land by the speculators. But in those days all who were settled on the land could produce good crops and sell all they produced at good prices. Today a good crop is a calamity, and a drought a blessing which keeps prices up. The world of 1869 was very different from the world of 1934, but I am not so sure that the world of 1934 is not in the long run the healthier. Already I could see signs of the orderly planning of agriculture in California. For many years the planters and growers had been organized into producers' cartels or co-operatives, to control the quantities of fruit put on the markets. Now I found that the activities of these private combines were being linked up with the Agricultural Adjustment Act, and the Federal Department of Agriculture in Washington had sanctioned the right of the combines to control the output of fruit, and the quantities and grades that enter the markets, and consequently the wholesale prices. California seems to be the only State in the Union where marketing by associations of producers, 100 per cent organized, is in full operation. The Californian fruit-growers are far more advanced in the matter of co-operative marketing than our fruit-growers in England. This may be because they are a compact body of people living in one irrigated plain, and working large plantations. With us in England our growers are scattered about all over the country, on holdings ranging from one acre to 500 acres.

The Californian fruit-growers have battled with adversity to some effect. Their marketing schemes cover apples, pears, apricots, peaches, plums and grape-fruit. Through their activities the cash income of the growers was increased by twenty million dollars for the season 1934. Surplus crops are kept off the markets and destroyed, and the owners are compensated from levies on the sales of the rest of the crop. I asked why this surplus could not be sent to feed the unemployed and destitute in the cities of the East instead of being destroyed, and I was told that this was being done. Why should the United States of America not feed its surplus population on its surplus crops?

On November 6th we were taken out for an all-day motor-trip by one of the staff of the Giannini Institute. He first took us southwards along the coastal plain, to see the orchards of peach, apricot, plum and apple, and afterwards to the forests of the coast range. We passed through miles of little villages of white, flat-roofed houses with wooden verandas, their Catholic churches with their little campanili, and here and there the sombre outline of a Protestant church or chapel. All this country was colonized first by settlers from Mexico, but later the wave of Anglo-Saxon Protestant migration came in from the East over the Rocky Mountains. The North American stock seems to predominate in these villages now, though all the names are Spanish still.

The weather, though it was November, was hot. There is no rain along this coast from April till December, and most of the orchard and garden crops have to be raised by irriga-tion. But the winter is so mild that along the foothills of the Coast Range, where irrigation is impossible, they can grow vegetables and some cereal crops by sowing in the autumn and harvesting in the spring. The crops grow in the mild winter rains and ripen when the warmth of spring arrives. The fruit-farms in the plains to the south of San Francisco are all from 50 to 150 acres in extent. They nestle picturesquely in little hollows, surrounded by groves of poplar, or nearer the hills they peep out from amidst the natural woodland of oak and pine, their orchards lying on the flats where irrigation canals can be cut. The houses are like wooden Swiss chalets, with store-rooms for boxes and the storage of fruit. Life must be pleasant in this land where Nature is kind and hospitable, but the growers with whom I came into contact were worried. The prices received for their fruit had been better, but they had had to reduce their output. No new plantings had been undertaken for two years. Indeed, we saw some old orchards which had been allowed to become derelict. But in spite of the decrease of acreage the output of fruit from this part of California was greater than it was two years ago. Modern methods of fruit-growing were increasing the yield per tree. Increasing output, decreasing foreign markets, the home market uncertain and not yet organized! The Californian fruit-grower has still need of courage.

We reached the Pacific coast at noon, and lunched at Santa Cruz. I noticed the display of fruit in the wayside shops. The apples were extremely poor. It seemed curious that in this land of fruit there should be no good apples for sale. The fact seemed to be that all the best are sent away, and only the inferior grades are sold in the district. The bulk of the first grade apples seem to go to England and the chief American cities of the East. We now struck northwards, and entered one of the coast ranges that run from Monterey Bay to San Francisco. These rise to about 1,500 feet, and in their deep valleys the giant redwood forests are to be seen. The famous giant redwood is *Sequoia sempervirens*, a very tall species with pectinate leaves. It grows in the mountain ranges which skirt the Pacific, at no great altitude, but it finds conditions here suitable, thanks to the constant mist and fog which come in from the ocean, and the deep valleys which protect it from the hot summer sun. It is characteristic of these low coast ranges that the southern slopes, facing the sun, are dry and bare, while on the northern side, in the deep valleys, the giant redwood forests grow, with scattered Douglas firs. We visited one of these valleys. The redwood grows to a tremendous height. I estimated that some of the trees were 250 feet in height, to the first branch being over 100 feet from the ground. The hot sun outside was quite excluded, and you found yourself under a great cool canopy, with giant wooden pillars rising up all round you. We could see where ages ago a great fire had swept the forest, when some of the old giants had been burnt to the heart and had died. But the bark of this tree is non-inflammable and protects the sapwood. In many cases it grew over the fire scar, and it is impossible to count the rings on the new growth. In this way it has been possible to determine just when the forest fires occurred. One can say that this tree was burnt in the time of Montezuma, but still lives, that this tree was scarred when the first Spanish Conquistadores came up from Mexico. Here is history written on trees!

We found here a Civil Conservation Camp which has been started under a Federal Relief Scheme. Unemployed men were working here, living during the week in these camps. They assist the forest rangers, help to clear away rubbish, fell trees where necessary, and watch for forest fires. Since they have been working the forest fires have been practically eliminated.—The men go home for the week-end. Their homes may be perhaps 200 miles distant, but that is nothing for this country. They receive their keep, and a portion of their pay goes to their families. The United States is fortunate in one sense. She has enormous forests which badly need workers to assist the rangers and forest officers. Lack of such workers has meant untold damage to natural resources in the past. The great forests of North America need the unemployed to come and preserve them. No wonder that public opinion in some States of America does not favour the payment of relief benefits, but insist on work being found on national development schemes. If only we had a few million acres of virgin forests in England for our unemployed to work in!

On November 8th we made an excursion to the north of San Francisco Bay, to Mount Tamalpais. We crossed the Golden Gate by ferry and visited the Muir Forest of redwoods. Here is the wonderful Cathedral Grove. In this awe-inspiring place you stand in a silent natural hall of ancient, growing timber. Then we ascended Mount Tamalpais (3,000 feet). Thence we looked westwards, and saw the Pacific Ocean at our feet. We saw no water: only a dense white mist, like a sea of cotton-wool, with islands of forested land rising out of it. We heard the fog-horns booming on the coast. This was the normal Pacific Coast fog, which rises out of the sea day after day and gently sweeps in towards the land, dispersing in the hot plains behind San Francisco. Away to the north and east we could see the coastal range and the foothills of the Sierra Nevada rising out of the irrigated lands, where tropical fruit is grown, but which are now dry, hard and yellow in the hot autumn sun. On our way back, recrossing the Golden Gate by ferry, we saw the great mist sweep inland over the Bay, and as it did not rise more than fifty feet above the water we saw the sky-scrapers of San Francisco rising out of the mist like a phantom city. California is indeed a land of dreams.

CHAPTER VIII

NATIONAL PARKS, LOS ANGELES AND THE GRAND CAÑON

WE left San Francisco on the night of November 8th, crossing the Bay by steamer to Oakland, where we took the night train to the South. Next morning we found ourselves in a small provincial town in the great central plain of California. The Pacific lay fifty miles to the west, and all around was a flat plain of irrigated fields. There were orchards of peaches, apricots, walnuts, plums and apples almost as far as the eye could see, with occasional breaks of fields in which grew tropical vegetables like egg-plant, chili, avocado, and other edible plants which I have never seen or heard of before. We saw one peach orchard which was 1,000 acres in extent! At every station on the railway there was a canning and packing plant, with a timber-yard for supplying material for the cases. They were owned by the different co-operative associations of growers. We stopped in the little town of Merced. As in other Californian towns, the buildings were Spanish and Oriental in type, like the vegetation, while the people were apparently of pure North American stock. Life seemed very quiet and comfortable here. America is everywhere a wonderful country for conveniences. Even in the small provincial towns you will find cafeterias to provide cheap meals, two or three cinemas to amuse you, a library, and travel agencies which will give you all the information that you can possibly want, and accurate information too. The young people that we saw in such towns looked keen, intelligent, and energetic, in spite of the warm climate. There did not seem to be much Latin blood in their veins.

From Merced we took the bus which runs to the Yosemite

Valley once a day. The route went eastwards across the plain, towards the Sierra Nevada. After a while we passed out of the irrigated orchard land into a region of low rolling hills. Here Hereford cattle were raised for beef on ranches which looked typical of the sort of thing you read about in Zane Grey's novels. Everything was true to type except the murderous villain, the handsome cowboy hero, and the lovely heroine. All these were conspicuous by their absence on the ranches we passed. In their place some worried rancher and his plump, middle-aged wife might be wondering if the price of heifers would enable him to meet his bank overdraft!

Presently the hills were higher, and even ranching slowly petered out. Trees appeared, first of all Digger Pine on the shady side of the hills, and then in the valley bottoms the Western Yellow or Heavy Pine. We stopped for a while at the village of Mariposa. This was a great mining settlement in the Gold Rush days. Now it consists of petrol pumps, garages, dumps for old iron and old Ford cars, a post-office, and the usual grocer's store. After this the country became mountainous. We were entering the Sierra Nevada. Forests of Heavy and Digger Pine covered the mountain-sides. We went down a precipitous road and entered into the narrow gorge of the Merced River. After another hour we saw in front of us enormous cliffs rising precipitously on both sides of the valley. A chain across the road halted our bus. A United States Federal Park and Forest officer—a typical clean-shaven American with a broad-brimmed hat— checked the contents of the bus, and we entered the Yose-mite National Park. The sight that now met us is not easy to describe. Imagine a Gustave Doré picture of Dante enter-ing the Inferno! Enormous cliffs seemed to close round us as we entered the narrow portal, but it would have been a libel to compare the place to the Inferno once we were inside, for the valley bottom opened out into the most idyllic natural parkland that one could possibly imagine. Giant Heavy Pines and Sugar Pines towered over us. Then came a tract of natural meadow; then a view of a river, rushing over cascades; and then a little lake. The sun shone fitfully, although there was not a cloud in the sky. We passed the famous El Capitan cliff. It rises sheer, 3,600 feet from the valley floor to its crest. Next we passed the Cathedral Cliffs, two pinnacles rising 1,000 feet, and ending in sharp needle-points. Then we approached the settlement, which contains the Park offices—a small Indian village, with a few rather miserable specimens of Indians, a very fine museum, a post-office, and an hotel. From this, the Ahwanee Hotel, we got a magnificent view of the Half Dome Rock. This is about 2,000 feet in height, and the top is like a rounded dome cut in half. All the afternoon we wandered about the valley. We visited the Yosemite Falls. These are 2,300 feet in height, but are broken at one spot, 2,000 feet from the top. They are the loftiest falls in the world, although there is a fall in British Guiana which is a close competitor.

At large in the park, wandering about under the great pines, were wild bears, which, however, were half tame. This park is an animal sanctuary, and we came across some five or six old bears, lumbering about under the trees and looking at us with their sly little eyes. They can be fed from the hand, but are often rough, and given to scratching, so that the keepers advise the public to throw food to them. The atmosphere of the valley was unlike anything else that I had felt before. Shut in by the huge cliffs, the air was completely still and almost sultry. The sun shone through the great gaps in the cliffs on to the natural park of meadow and pine-clumps. It was all just as Nature had made it. Man had only tidied it up, making Nature a little neater. There was almost complete silence in the valley but for the occasional cry of a blue jay or the faint swish of the Yosemite Falls. I kept on comparing our experience in this lovely valley with that of my father in 1869. To reach it he had ridden on horseback for two or three days, and had then put up in a log hut. He had hunted wild sheep in the thickets, which had escaped from an Indian tribe, and had cooked his own food. Moreover, the Indian tribes were none too friendly then, and the white man was not a permanent resident in the valley. Now you buy your ticket from any agent; you are brought here in luxurious buses, stay in a hotel that has a bathroom for every guest, with hot and cold water laid on, elegant lounges and cocktail bars, and cars to take you everywhere, so that you need not walk a yard— and no American ever does seem to walk anywhere. I must say that I felt a little uneasy at all this luxury, and longed for a little of the old type of travel, and to ride on horseback occasionally, or walk a mile or two. In travelling the enjoyment of the sights one sees is enhanced by the difficulty in getting to them. Ease of access tends to reduce one's interest. The revolution in transport since my father's day has revolutionized travel and the mode of enjoying it. I foresee a horrifying picture of the next generation, taking all their pleasures in motor-cars and armchairs. On the other side of the account it must be said that the Yosemite Valley is a magnificent example of a great natural beauty-spot, preserved for ever for the public, and I think the Federal Government's work in tending Nature and tidying without altering it is beyond all praise. It is the finest and best organized national park I have ever seen, but it is not the only one of its kind on this continent. The Americans have developed the making and keeping of national parks to a fine art, and no other country can touch them in this respect. Moreover, it is satisfactory to note that in the Yosemite all classes of people are catered for, and not only the rich. There are excellent camping-grounds and huts for those whose means are limited, and cheap rooms in hostels for parties of working-folk. The general tone of the visitors to the park is high. They are being educated to conduct themselves properly. Most excellent educational facilities are provided by talented young University men, who give lectures on the geology, flora, fauna and history of the park. In the museum I learnt that the theory held as to the origin of the valley in my father's time, and to which he refers in his letters, is superseded. The valley was carved out by glacial action. The great dome-shaped cliffs are probably connected with the molten granite beneath the earth's crust, which has cooled into gigantic nodules, and these on erosion peel off like the skins of an onion.

On November 11th we arrived in the early morning at Los Angeles. This is a unique city. It is really the largest of a whole chain of towns and settlements which are scattered for thirty miles down this part of the Pacific coast. Situated amidst gently undulating hills and valleys above the blue waters of the Pacific, it enjoys a perfect climate of almost everlasting summer. Needless to say, it attracts settlers from all over the world. Old people with means go there to end their days in an American Riviera. Retired business people go there for society and the many sports and pastimes which can be found there, such as yachting, riding, racing, polo, and fishing. But most important of all, it includes, as one of its satellite towns, Hollywood, where the world's greatest film industry has its headquarters. The presence of this film industry attracts to Los Angeles from all over the world all manner of men and women who have, or think they have, any possible prospect of being employed on the films. Mechanics seeking work in the studios wait in numbers for the first job that offers. Perhaps a film is being produced in which someone is needed who speaks the language of a South Sea Island. A notice in the local Press will produce a score of the qualified actors who have been waiting their chance. Poverty there is in Los Angeles in plenty, and a great amount of unemployment, or rather of under employment, but even poverty is mitigated by the beautiful climate and the relative cheapness of food, including good vegetables and fruit. The vote given to Upton Sinclair in Los Angeles was indicative of unrest, but those who voted for him were not wholly or even mainly the poorer section of the community. In many cases they were artisans and mechanics who were earning good money at the studios, or in some of the small industries which have come from the East in recent years. Evidently a large minority of the population of Los Angeles think that, in spite of ideal climate and cheap food, society is too chaotic to provide them with security of livelihood. And security is the one thing that the average man most needs today.

In Los Angeles we called on a German doctor who, because he was a Jew, had been compelled to leave Nazi Germany, although he had fought for Germany in the war. He had sadly turned his face from the Old World and his cultural home, and had taken refuge in the great unknown world of America. Although America had welcomed him to her shores as a distinguished physician, I don't think he felt at ease in his new country. He was still longing for Germany—if not for the new, at least for the old Germany. He had not been long enough in the country to have been influenced by its elusive, absorbing atmosphere. A colleague of his, a former Russian Jew, who had lived in America for forty years, was an example of what he will probably become one day, if he lives long enough. This man still had an academic sympathy for the Old World, whose civilization is now in danger of falling into decay under the influence of war and economic collapse and their consequence, Fascism. He had followed the developments of Russian Communism, and had tried to understand it as a native product of Eastern Europe and Western Asia. But when I questioned him as to his ideas respecting the future of America, I found that he regarded the Atlantic as an insulating barrier. Neither Fascism nor Communism, he said, would come to America; great social changes there would be in the United States, and possibly upheavals, but the liberty of the individual and of the rights of free speech would be respected. Forty years had turned him from a potential East European rebel into a member of the great band of intelligent American Liberals. The great American melting-pot had fused him into its common alloy.

From Los Angeles we drove down to the coast through Hollywood, where we saw the film stars' villas and the studios, surrounded by great walls. In the restaurants we saw interesting types of people from all over the world, most of them either in the employ of the studios, or hoping against hope to be employed there, and meanwhile living on charity or their friends. Along the coast we saw the effects of speculation and the land boom. Great spaces had been fenced off by land companies and made ready for development. But then the crash came, and now the weeds are growing taller each year. The local government of these Pacific coast towns is relatively free from corruption. Because they are comparatively new the Irish professional politician has been unable to establish Tammany there. The churches seem to have taken the place of Tammany as the dominating influence in local politics. No one can get on the municipal council of Los Angeles unless he has the support of the church leaders and has satisfied them on the drink and school questions. In this respect I think we are better off in England. We have no Irish to trouble us now and the churches have long been put in their proper place.

We took the day train on November 12th to visit the Grand Cañon of Arizona. It was pleasant to view the orange and grape-fruit orchards as the train passed the irrigated belt to the east of Los Angeles. But in this land of contrasts we had soon reached the other extreme of aridity. We were approaching the dry uplands of Arizona, which are never reached by the moisture-laden winds from the Pacific. Here we saw for the first time cactus growing on wide expanses. At wayside stations we saw Spanish or Mexican cowboys, true to type and wearing the real sombrero hat and cowboy costume. Indians too appeared at Needles, the station where the line crosses the Colorado River. Night came, and the train puffed up the incline, steadily rising until we were nearly 7,000 feet above sea-level. We were shunted off on to a branch line, and next morning found ourselves at a small terminus.

We walked from the station to a hotel close by. It was built of logs in the middle of a forest of scrub pine. We went into the coffee-room for breakfast, and when we looked out from the window we stood and gasped. We realized that the hotel was built on the edge of the Grand Cañon, of which nothing can be seen until you arrive at the very edge. One felt like a fly that had crawled across a table until it had suddenly come to the edge. The Yosemite valley was an idyll, a dream come true, Elysian fields of gigantic proportions, but the Grand Cañon is the most overwhelming sight I have ever seen. It is grim, almost terrifying. For in this one spot on all the earth Nature allows Man to look 4,000 feet into her bosom. There is beauty as well as terror here, but one's first and most abiding impression is of the overpowering forces of Nature. One cannot adequately describe the spectacle. Someone has written of it: "Most people are dumb when they see it, as if they were in the presence of Nature's Sacrament."

To see this great sight fully would have taken several days. We could have ridden down into the chasm on horses, gone up the Bright Angel Trail, visited the Indian settlements and seen the cataracts of the Colorado River. Travellers in the United States have to make a decision early on in their journey. If they are going to travel simply for pleasure and recreation, they can visit only a few places and spend much time there, ride horses, camp out, and live the life of the modern cultural pioneer in this wonderful country. But if they do this, they cannot cover the whole country, unless they have months of time at their disposal. If they are bent on gathering material and learning something of the American people in all their divers occupations, or noting their reactions in the throes of great social and economic crises, they cannot play the holiday-maker. They must push on from place to place, interview, visit, question, and collect material, seizing only such opportunities for sight-seeing as their other plans will allow. Of course, with a little arrangement one can manage to do a certain amount of sight-seeing, but one must cut out the delight, horse-riding and camping in America's great National Parks. In our case we contented ourselves with a day's motor tour along the rim of the Grand Cañon. This really enabled us to see a great deal from various points of vantage, and we could probably read the geological history of the great Cañon better than if we had ridden down into the chasm. And everything was well organized, as are all the sight-seeing and educational tours in America. Trained geologists met us and explained to us all we wanted to know. Telescopes were ready for us to scan the gorge. Museums were dotted here and there. The American genius for efficient organization was here seen at its best.

The Grand Cañon is formed by the Great Colorado River, which has cut a gorge in the earth's crust 217 miles in length, ten miles in width, and on an average about a mile in depth! It has taken a thousand million years to do this and it is hard at work still, for as fast as it cuts its way down, the level of the earth's crust slowly rises and the gulley grows deeper and deeper. It is the combination of river erosion, gradual earth-crust elevation, and (in my opinion) the relatively dry atmosphere, which minimizes side-wash, that has made this wonderful chasm. The earth's history is here revealed from the black granite gorges, like the depths of Dante's Inferno, down which the Colorado River plunges, through the earliest sedimentary rocks, about 2,000 feet thick, that lie above them, through the great coal-measure period, which is here represented by strata only a few feet thick, either because there was no land here in that age, or because the coal deposits were washed away in the period immediately following, down to great blown sand deposits of the later Permian and Mezozoic ages, where one can find the footprints of gigantic Dinosaurs. These monsters lived a few thousand million years ago, but they appear only in the uppermost or latest of the Grand Cañon strata. Indeed, most of their remains lie in the "Painted Desert" to the east of the Cañon. Two-thirds of the earth's history is revealed in the Cañon. The remaining third is but yesterday.

Later in the day we motored forty miles eastward to the spot where the Cañon makes a great bend. Coming down from the north, it sweeps at right angles to the west. Here we climbed an old Indian watch-tower, which has been recently restored. To the west and north rose weird pinnacles of rock in fantastic shapes, like Mexican Aztec temples, Chinese pagodas and Indian shrines. Here and there we could see the bottom of the gorge, where the Colorado

River was plunging between black granite walls. It carries a million tons of débris with it to the sea in twenty-four hours. On its raging flood venturesome souls have from time to time gone down in boats, trying to shoot the rapids. But the river has taken a heavy toll of those that have dared. Eastwards we looked across the "Painted Desert." There lay a great expanse of flat tableland, and here and there layers of rocks and sandstone protruded from the desert floor like huge table-tops. The eye followed the desert contours to the very borders of New Mexico, where a snow-white peak of the Southern Rockies gleamed faintly bluish-white through the haze. We saw mirages, streaks of red, yellow and purple, as the evening sun illuminated the terraced layers of the desert. Here and there I thought I could make out the mud huts and encampments of the Navajo Indians. Then the sun went down on the Grand Cañon, the evening glow faded out, and an opaque darkness enveloped this great wonder of Nature in the cloak of night. Returning to railhead, we went to an Indian house and watched some members of the Hopi tribe do the Eagle and other dances. Then we got into the train and slept, seeing visions of earthly chasms, "painted deserts" and dancing Indians.

CHAPTER IX

NEW MEXICO—THE SPANISH-INDIAN FRINGE

JUST as we in England have our Celtic fringe, so the United States has its Spanish-Indian fringe on the South-West borderlands. In Wales and Scotland our Celts have blended with the Anglo-Saxon in that happy union which, while preserving all that is best in both races, has given added strength to the whole. Of the calamity of Anglo-Irish relations, however, the less said the better. What is the effect of the mingling of the two cultures of the New World in New Mexico, the last of the States to be admitted to the Union? And how is the native population in this part of the United States of America reacting to the new situation? That was the question of which we hoped to learn something as we sped along in the California Limited from the Arizona desert to the plateaux of the Rio Grande. It was soon clear that the aspect of the country was becoming more and more Spanish and Mexican. At the wayside stations and along the roads, which followed closely the railway, one saw the Mexican cowboy type and dress. The road traffic was a queer mixture: Americans of all sorts speeding east and west in cars across the great trunk road. There were tourists going to and from California, or business men travelling to and from the cities of the East to their depôts and branches out West. The same types were to be seen on the railways, with the addition of those members of the middle class, recently rendered poor by the depression, who could not afford to run a motor-car.

How well the trunk roads were laid and appointed. Halting-stations and garages at intervals, signals flashing at night, like lighthouses in the desert, to tell the driver his whereabouts. And on the hillsides great letters painted in white on the rock to give the pilots of aeroplanes their bearings. The railways have not only the road to compete with now, but the airways also. It is little wonder that one never has any difficulty in booking a berth on a trans-continental train, and that most of the railway companies can do no more than pay the interest on their bonds; and not all can do even this.

The villages were at first Mexican, the language spoken Spanish, and the religion Roman Catholic. The people were descended from the followers of the Spanish military rulers who conquered this province in the early days. Dark-eyed, dark-haired, typical Spaniards, they were cultivators of corn and fruit on the irrigated lands and raisers of live-stock on the dry, stony uplands, as their fathers were. They had full American citizenship, and all spoke some English. Presently we passed the first Indian villages. These were the homes of the "Pueblo" Indians, as the Mexicans call them—that is, the Indians who live in "pueblos" or villages, as distinct from those further north and west who live mainly in tents. These are the Indians who came early under Spanish influence and learnt agriculture and the use of horses from the Spaniards, thus settling down to village and farm life soon after the white men came to the continent, though they probably practised primitive agriculture before the white man came.

We stopped at a place called Isleta and left the train in order to visit the Indian village of that name. The village consisted of flat-roofed houses made of adobe—hard, sun-baked clay. The Indians were typical redskins, with hooked noses, jet-black eyes, and coarse black hair, which was cut in a fringe over the eyes. The dress was much less Indian in character than I had expected. The influence of the modern textile industry was in evidence; the shirts worn

M   177

by the men and women had been made in the New England factories. But the women's garments had evidently been dyed locally to suit the Indian taste for bright and well-matched colours. For coats the men wore woollen blankets wrapped round the shoulder. These had come from the Navajo Indians in Arizona, and many were tastefully coloured. The Pueblo Indians' handwork was mainly jewellery. Every village we saw contained a few households engaged in working up turquoises from the mines in the Rocky Mountains and Mexico, embedding them in silver and encrusting them in every conceivable sort of design. Like the Mexicans, the Pueblo Indians were growing corn and fruit and grazing livestock. Those near the railway were not hunters, but those we visited later near the mountains still kept up their ancient livelihood of fur-hunting, though the proceeds of this occupation are much smaller than they used to be. The men were mostly of fine physique, though some tended to fat, and the same qualification applies to the women, even to those who had reached only a moderate age. My impression was that they were not lazy, as are the degenerate types which we had seen in the North. These Indians have evidently been able to assimilate, to a certain extent, the habits and ways of living of the Spaniards, and then of the Americans, without becoming demoralized. They have learnt agriculture and metal-working from the whites, but in other respects they have retained their Indian culture. The only sign of demoralization that I saw in Isleta was among the Indian children; dreadful little brats, who had evidently been spoiled by contact with tourists.

We visited the Roman Catholic church in Isleta; it is about a hundred and fifty years old, and contains some fine old sacred pictures brought from Europe. A face of Christ, with markedly Jewish features, is said to have been painted in the Middle Ages in Rome. This church, which figures in the famous novel, *Death Comes to the Archbishop*, was a monument of the European culture, religion and art which were transplanted in unchanged form to the American continent, and offered, often forcibly, to the Indians. There it stood uncompromisingly—*Semper eadem*. What influence for good or evil has it had on the life and culture of the Indians? Not very much, I think, for the art of agriculture and the handicrafts were not necessarily connected with religion, although the missionaries taught them. The Indians could have learnt them without Roman Catholicism. Indeed, as we observed later, Christianity seemed to have had little more effect on the Pueblos than water on a duck's back.

Continuing by car to Albuquerque, we found it a typical Spanish-American provincial town, with an American veneer of chain-stores, petrol stations and old car dumps. It was not picturesque, and showed that the Mexicans and the Americans are coming together in their joint industrial and commercial enterprises and in the mode of building their houses. The Americans are active mainly as administrators and business men. We saw a few white American ranching stations along the roads and railways, and further away towards the hills, which we visited later. Further south there are fruit plantations owned and worked by white Americans, but these we did not see. The Americans are in a minority, but a casual glance at such towns as Albuquerque shows that they are the dominating economic influence. The depression has hit the provincial towns in these parts as severely as elsewhere. I heard of much money lost, and hard times for all, although wherever there are Americans there is always a certain breezy optimism in respect of the future, however bad the times may be. Incidentally, the local taxation system in the counties and townships of these Western States seems a curious one to our English notions.

If a man has a business which does not pay, and he closes it down in a depression, he still has to pay taxes, even if it is a derelict shell. Anyone who buys a business or land out here must first ascertain what taxes are due on it, or he may find himself on the road to ruin. Here is proof of America's great weakness: lack of good local administration in general and local taxation in particular. There is no properly trained local civil service.

We alighted from the train on the afternoon of November 14th at the wayside station of Lamy, and there took the bus for Santa Fé, the State capital of New Mexico, about twenty-five miles to the north. The city of Santa Fé is situated on the edge of hills covered with scrub forest. It is high up on a plateau through which the Rio Grande flows on its way from the Rockies to the sea. It is almost on the southern limits of the Rockies. A stony desert plateau lies around the town. Santa Fé is watered by a stream from the hills which flows in irrigation canals, through groves of poplars, to the gardens and orchards. The flat-roofed adobe houses are typically Oriental in appearance. A superficial glance, however, showed us that the town was very Spanish. The smaller shops and businesses, the artisan and working classes, were Spanish. The larger business houses from the East had depôts there, and these were staffed by Anglo-Saxon Americans; and the administrators in the State offices were also largely English-speaking. One quarter of the city, the least attractive part of it, contained the State offices and the Legislature of New Mexico. These were rather inferior imitations of the Capitol in Washington, and completely out of place. What a pity they did not build a Parliament House in the style of the native architecture of Spanish America! Yet what a change from the days when my father visited Santa Fé in 1878! Then the Governor, his officials, and the garrison of a handful of officers and troopers were all quartered in the old one-storied, flat-roofed Spanish Government House. This is now the State Museum, and the seat of government is shifted to inferior imitations of the classical style. The old grass-covered Plaza of my parents' days is now a boulevard, with modern shops surrounding the square. Where mules were once tied, and Indians lounged about, are petrol pumps, depôts of Standard Oil, chain-stores, Woolworths, and Ford garages. Modern America is fast changing the face of this ancient Hispano-Indian land.

We went to the fine La Fonda Hotel. Here the owners have adapted a native style of building, providing all modern improvements and comforts. Indeed, even in the remotest places the American hotels are uniformly good, and to our English standards luxurious. Baths and telephones in every room seem to us the height of luxury. We found at this hotel that a great conference of the Highway Officials of the United States was being held. At night there was dancing and singing in the big lounge. Everybody who was somebody in Santa Fé, and probably some who weren't, was present. The company was predominantly Spanish. The Spanish business people, and the Spanish elements in the local administration, many of them the descendants of the old, now extinct, Mexican aristocracy, had turned out for the occasion. Union with the United States meant for this province of Old Mexico a general social levelling of all classes, much to the advantage of everybody. The Anglo-Saxon Americans were there in smaller numbers. I met the editor of the local newspaper, a charming American of Irish descent, who was also secretary to Senator Capper, representing New Mexico in the Federal Senate. I had a long talk with him on the politics and problems of this part of America, while Spanish musicians played "O Sole mio" and Spanish songs on guitars and mandolins, and dark-haired caballeros and dusky señoritas danced the tango before admiring onlookers. In this atmosphere of smoke, music, and reverie I found it hard to realize that I was still in the United States, and marvelled at the diversity of this great land. My mind went back to the ball given in honour of General Sherman in this very town, fifty-six years ago, which my parents attended. The only society then was provided by the officers of the United States garrison and their wives and the old Mexican aristocracy. I felt that this was a more democratic gathering. The spirit of the Declaration of Independence had been doing its work in the intervening years. For here and there among the crowd could be seen brightly dressed Indians from the pueblos, who had come in to see the fun, and to sell their jewels and embroideries. And something else struck me too. The people here have not been spoilt by jazz. The democratic social levelling has not demoralized art. The Spanish people here have kept their native dance and music with a tenacity which is above all praise.

At the same time, I did not find among the Spaniards with whom I talked any signs of distinctive national feeling. They were citizens of the United States, and seemed quite content to be so. Their Spanish nationalism was cultural only, and the Latin element was contributing its share to the common life of the continent, as the Scotch, Welsh, and English contribute to the common life of the British Isles. The burning questions of the day in New Mexico cut right across national and racial lines. When my parents were here the great question was how to pacify the Indians, how to suppress them, if necessary, and keep the Spanish people neutral in the struggle with the Indian tribes. Today the question is how to raise the earning power of the cultivators and stock-breeders and graziers, whose income had been affected by the drop in prices; the problem I had encountered elsewhere, only in different surroundings. There was not much unemployment in this agrarian land, but a good deal of poor living, for the methods of farming were antiquated. Dependence on cash crops and livestock for the packing stations had made the agricultural economy one-sided. Spanish and Indian cultivators and stock-raisers were being asked to try a more self-sufficing maintenance type of farming. In particular the Navajo Indians to the west of Santa Fé have overgrazed their lands, so that soil erosion has become a grave problem. These Indians are increasing in numbers, being a strong and virile race. Liberal Republicans like Senator Capper and others have been trying to induce them to accept the advice of the United States Federal experts as to new methods of cropping grass, the better to support the increasing tribal population. Recently these efforts, backed by the Federal Government, have met with success.

But as usual in this country, I found that the altruistic work of certain public-spirited men and women was being complicated by the wire-pulling and graft of the party caucuses. Just at the time of our arrival there was a first-class row in progress concerning the recent election for the Federal Senate and the local legislature. The Republican and Democratic Senatorial candidates had apparently identical programmes of conditional support for the New Deal. But the managers of the two party machines were less concerned with this than with the control of jobs which electoral victory would give them. Accordingly Santa Fé was ringing with accusations and counter-accusations of bribery and corruption. From what I could hear, many of the accusations were justified. New Mexican politics has been notoriously corrupt, judged even by United States standards, and it would not surprise me, should the conduct of elections here ever become the subject of public inquiry, to hear that Washington had decided to disenfranchise the State for a time. From all accounts, the electoral ethics and manners of New Mexico are comparable to those of the famous Eatanswill election!

Next day (November 15th) we went to visit some Indian and Spanish villages off the beaten track. We drove off in a car with a small and jolly party of Americans, ascending the valley of the Rio Grande. The river seemed a shallow rippling stream at this time of year, threading its way through poplar brakes and irrigated paddocks of maize, melon gardens, and orchards of plum and apple. Sage and wiry grass grew where the irrigation canals did not water the soil. In the middle distance rose mountain ranges, with here and there a touch of autumn snow on their heights. I was strongly reminded of similar scenes in Central Asia. Soon we entered a gorge of the Rio Grande, and the river began to run more rapidly. We followed the road on to a high plateau, 7,000 feet above the sea. Here there was a Spanish village, with a very old Catholic church. In the market-place we stopped and walked about among typical Mexican cowboys. It was delightful to find people who actually still ride horses. Here were Mexicans who had ridden in from ranches at the foot of the mountains, driving cattle to market, and were now buying stores for the week, instead of motoring to town over the stony desert and shipping off their cattle in lorries. In some respect this part of New Mexico had not changed very much since my father and mother were here.

About a mile beyond the Spanish market town we came to the Indian village of Taos, nestling under a range of forested mountains. It is one of the most perfect of the Indian pueblos in existence, and is just as it was in the days when the Spaniards came in 1480. It is, however, unique in one respect—it is the only village in which there are five tiers of flat-roofed houses, laid one on top of the other, like so many boxes, and in which you approach the upper houses from the roofs of the lower. Many of the houses were accessible only through holes in the roof, through which one descended on ladders. There are other villages with three tiers of houses but none with five. The Pueblo Indians of New Mexico are the only Indians who have retained this mode of building their villages, which were originally designed for defence against other Indian tribes in the days before the coming of the Spaniards. The Indians in Old Mexico and in the South American Republics, like Peru and Bolivia, have abandoned this type of building, so that this village of Taos, and a few others in New Mexico, are unique in character. Indeed the Indians in Mexico proper are now impure and largely intermarried with Mexicans. These Pueblo Indians are the purest on the continent.

We found this Indian village much less influenced by the outside world than others we had seen. There is now every opportunity for the Indians to preserve their own culture. Their rights are most carefully respected. We found the elected chief in his house, with a wand of office given originally by Abraham Lincoln, who first initiated the system. We found that the chief had absolute control over the families in the village, and the Federal Courts have no jurisdiction over civil disputes between Indians. Only in the case of infringements of the criminal law between an Indian and a white American could the Federal Courts exercise their authority. We found that the Indians pay no taxes, but do not vote. Their land is guaranteed to them by the President for ever, so that no American or Spaniard can touch it. Education too is free, the cost being defrayed by the Federal Governmant. Medical and nursing services are provided at very small cost. Altogether I had the impression that the Indians are being almost pampered. What is

being done today seems to be in the nature of conscience
money to make amends for the scandalous way in which
the Indians were treated in the past, first by the Spaniards,
who killed them to save their souls for the Catholic Church,
and later by the American pioneers, who enslaved them to
exploit their bodies for the Almighty Dollar. I had a talk
with one Indian, whose house I entered, and in the course
of conversation I remarked on the great apparent improvement in the relations between Indians and whites. But it
does not seem that these sad and dreadful memories linger
now, except perhaps in the recesses of the Indian brain. For
when I spoke in this strain he seemed almost surprised to
think that there had ever been a racial war between Red and
White. I could see that it was an effort for him to remember
the facts of the Indian uprising against the Spaniards in the
seventeenth century, and against the Americans in 1867,
with the consequent repression.

Walking about Taos we saw the little Catholic church
at one end of the village, but at the other end we saw something far more interesting. This was the "Kiwa," or underground secret chamber, fenced round by a stockade,
approached by a ladder, and marked by two long poles
protruding above the ground. In this underground chamber
pre-Christian religious rites are carefully performed under
the supervision of the village chief. The Catholic priests
cannot stop them, and do not try to do so now, for these
people are only superficially Catholic, and under the mask
of Catholicism they carry on their old religion, which is
the worship of the spirits of Nature. For instance, the
Thunder Bird when he claps his wings causes thunder in
the heavens, and this brings rain; so he is looked upon as
sacred; and very naturally the thunderstorms, which are
the outward and visible sign of the Thunder Bird, are
sacred to the Indians, because they are the chief source of

rain in this country. Then, again, the Bear is the spirit of Evil. The Eagle is the spirit of the Forest, which gives them timber and wild animals and furs. When one looks upon the Indian religion as a projection into the mystical of the age-long struggle of this people to win the fruits of the earth, one is glad to find that they have retained their ancient faith. Of course, a certain amount of rank superstition is found intermingled with this sane and rational worship of the spirits of Nature. For instance, there is the snake dance, when poisonous rattlesnakes are loosed and treated with the greatest veneration. Anyone who killed a rattlesnake would be left to die if ever he was bitten by one! (This has actually happened.) Many of these secret ceremonies may not be witnessed by white persons. But an American professor of anthropology who has lived with these Indians and has won their confidence has been allowed to see some of them. Of course, many of the dances are performed above ground, and the whites are allowed to see them, especially the dance which celebrates the gathering of the harvest, which has a deep religious significance. But one wonders how the Indians will react when they begin to realize modern economic problems. They have hitherto thanked their spirits for sending them good harvests. In future they will have to pray to their spirits to send them good markets, good prices, and money for the townspeople to buy their produce. They may in time pray to the great spirit in the White House in Washington to make the New Deal a success! But up to now the Indians have not tumbled to the great problem which confronts them, as it does all mankind, and they go on dancing and praying for good harvests, which with the world as it is today may only deepen their distress.

We were very favourably impressed by the Indians. The men were most dignified and courteous; Nature's gentlemen, in fact. But they were very reticent, and did not talk much. I had the impression, and our guide agreed, that they feel themselves superior to the whites. They regard themselves as the old American stock, and the only aristocracy of the continent. The dignity and sense of *noblesse oblige* which I noted in these Indian villages was in marked contrast with what I experienced in Turkestan, Eastern Russia, Asia Minor, and the Caucasus, when I visited Tartar or Turkoman encampments. These latter peoples regarded the whites as their equals only. At all events, one could walk about their villages without any excessive sense of deference. But in the Indian villages one felt that one was highly honoured to be allowed to come near the place. I felt like a country cousin who had come up to visit a duchess in a London drawing-room at the height of the season. The Pueblo Indian regards himself as America's Red aristocrat. On the other hand, according to all that I heard of them it seems that the Indians are most faithful friends if once you can win their confidence and respect.

I don't think they are very clever in the white man's sense of the word. I gathered that the school-children are fairly intelligent, as regards arithmetic and head work generally, but are on the whole slow. They probably have the country-man's slyness and extreme caution very highly developed. But they have not got the inferiority complex; rather the reverse! It will be interesting to see what happens if some of the younger generation, after obtaining an education which brings them to some extent into touch with American life, attempt on their return to change the patriarchal life of their native village. The problem is not acute as yet, but I heard of cases in which members of the younger generation were unwilling to return to the discipline of the tribe after tasting the relative freedom outside. I heard of an Indian servant-girl who worked for an American family in Santa

Fé, and was happy in her employment. But her tribal chief recalled her to her village for the sacred dances, and would not allow her to return. The discipline is so strict that she dared not disobey. She had learnt from the Americans cleanliness, efficient organization, the need to speak the truth, and presumably the desire to make money. She was loth to renounce this heady wine. Until recently the policy of the Federal Government has been to discourage the tribal customs and organizations, to break up the native society and give freedom to each Indian individual, on the basis of the literal interpretation of the American Constitution. This in times past meant freedom for the white man to exploit the Indian. But the modern policy is to preserve the native institutions. So Washington today protects the tribal democracy. But the danger of this policy is that it also protects the elected chiefs, who are often petty autocrats, and would make short work of any young Indians who returned to the tribe with new ideas gathered from the white American colleges. It seems that the United States may some day be faced with just the same problem which now exists in some of the British Crown Colonies, where the African, Hindu or Malayan native, educated in English schools and universities, returns home to find himself restricted politically by the British administrators and socially by the petty tyranny of the caste or tribe. But the problem is never likely to become so acute in the United States as in the British Empire, for the Red Indians constitute only a very small percentage of the population of the country. But I fancy this question is ripening, and may at any moment present an issue to the Federal authorities.

We found the educational and hygienic work which was being done in the pueblos by the white Americans beyond all praise. One great defect of pueblo life is that the Indians do not feed their children properly after they are two years

189

of age. They give them no milk, the dairy industry being almost non-existent. Infantile mortality among Indians is consequently high. Moreover, it is not easy for the Indians to change their mode of agriculture in such a way as to introduce the keeping of dairy cattle.

We returned to Santa Fé that evening. We had made in one day, and in a luxurious car, after enjoying a sumptuous if hotly spiced Spanish lunch at a wayside restaurant, a journey which took my father and mother two days and two nights to accomplish in an ambulance wagon! When they arrived in Santa Fé with General Sherman and his escort the guns boomed to herald their approach, and the Indians and Spaniards looked anxiously out of their houses to see what the great white men from the North were up to now. When we arrived in Santa Fé that evening the church bells were ringing, but not for us. When my parents stayed in Santa Fé they had to accept the hospitality of officers of the garrison and live on coffee and melon, served at unearthly hours. When we got back that night the gong at the La Fonda Hotel summoned us to a cheery meal of clam chowder soup, bluefish, Mexican quail and Californian fruits. I felt too pampered, and wished I could rough it a little, as in the old days.

Before we left Santa Fé we went to see the old Catholic church, founded by the friars in the seventeenth century. There we met a French priest who had been expelled from Mexico owing to the anti-Catholic campaign of the revolutionary government of that country. From my conversation with him and from other sources, I learned that there is a regular clerical emigré population, expelled from Mexico, and now living on the borders of the United States territory. This population is bitterly disaffected to the Mexican Government, and must be the cause of some embarrassment to the American authorities. I suppose,

190

like all emigrés, they will realize in time the hopelessness of the struggle for the ancient ecclesiastical privileges which have been abolished for good, and will settle down sooner or later as United States citizens. Mexico today has a new religion of social reconstruction.

CHAPTER X

DIXIELAND

WE now said good-bye to the great plains and plateaux of the West, the irrigated fruit gardens, Mexican cowboys, Catholic churches, and Indian pueblos. We had seen something of New England, the Middle West, the Rockies, the Pacific coast, and the Spanish-Indian country—five great cultural-economic areas of the United States. There still remained a sixth to be seen—Dixieland, the land of the negro and the cotton-fields. There are forty-eight States in the Union, but they are largely artificial divisions, drawn arbitrarily across the continent to represent old political boundaries. The real divisions are those I have mentioned above; the six Americas, each of which has its own special form of industry and agriculture, based on climate and geographical features, and its own special cultural and political outlook, and makes its own contribution to the formation of public opinion in the Federal Republic.

We left Santa Fé on the night of November 16th, taking the eastward-bound California Limited. In this we travelled as far as Kansas City, whence we made our detour to the South. We had resolved to cross the Mason-Dixon line and spend what time was left to us in studying the South.

On Sunday morning—a grey autumn day—the train from Kansas City arrived in St. Louis. Here we spent most of the day waiting for a train to the South. American provincial cities in the Middle West have few distinctive features and St. Louis is no exception. Even "Ole Man River" looked dull and drab on that November morning. The stern-paddle steamers had been tied up for the winter. We were too late in the year to see the busy life and the human ebb and flow that moves along the romantic and famous highway of the Mississippi. We soon realized, however, that we were coming into another America, whose customs and traditions were different from those of the Americas that we had seen. The negro porters at the station were more than usually friendly, chatty, pleasant, and unreliable. The beautiful smooth-running expresses that had carried us to and fro across the vast continent now gave place to an unpunctual, jolting and banging old train which carried us from St. Louis across Kentucky and Tennessee to the confines of picturesque Georgia. When we woke up on the morning of November 19th, and looked out of the window, we saw that we were really in Dixieland. There were pretty little hills and valleys with pine and oak forest, small scattered farms, and small fields of cotton and maize with negroes working in them. No one could be energetic in such a land. The little wooden houses, like untidy Swiss chalets, peeped out from behind clumps of pine-trees and disappeared as quickly as the train swung round a curve and brought a cotton-field in sight. Next a vista of oak forest appeared, and again a wooden hut in a clearing, where negro women in bright garments were scouring their maize-cobs. In such a land Hansel and Gretel might have wandered through the woods. How different from the great prairies out West, where the limitless prospect and exhilarating air seems to make everyone energetic! Presently we arrived in Atlanta, the capital of Georgia, known to me hitherto only as the place from which General Sherman made his famous march to the sea.

Atlanta seemed to me thoroughly out of place. It was just like the monotonous provincial cities that one sees in the Middle West. The explanation is, of course, that it represents the enterprising North America which invaded the dreamy but beautiful old South after the Civil War. But it seems that in recent years at least the South has begun to participate in this change, for much of the capital and industry here is now in the hands of Southerners, and many of the professional classes are Southerners whose fathers and grandfathers thought it beneath their dignity to lift a finger for themselves, or even to give an order to a slave except through an overseer.

After we had settled ourselves in Atlanta we went to see Dr. Alexander, one of the heads of the Inter-racial Commission which has been formed by Southern whites to fight for equality of rights for the negroes and to improve the relations between the races. We had a long talk with him, and were favourably impressed. Dr. Alexander and his colleagues are doing good work in the face of the prejudice which still survives. The greatest danger to good relations between the two races seems to be the discrimination against the negro in the industrial field. The depression has hit the South quite as badly as, if not worse than, any other part of the United States of America. And the white section of the working classes and the small farmers, or "poor whites," as they are called, are as bad as the professional classes and well-to-do whites in trying to shift the burden of the depression on to the shoulders of the coloured people, thereby intensifying race feeling. Negro workers get slung out of jobs to make room for whites, and when President Roosevelt offers the Southern States federal money to relieve unemployment, the Southern State legislators distribute the money so that the mere coloured man gets as little as possible of it. The reason given for this is that the negro standard of living is so low that the negroes need little or nothing, and can always go and catch a few fish in the rivers. Indeed, this is what I actually saw a little later in Georgia—namely, unemployed negroes sitting in rows at the riverside, trying to catch fish for their only meal in the day. The Inter-racial

Commission are fighting this sort of thing, but they have against them the demagogues who are such a terrible factor in American politics. It is the easiest thing in the world for a Southern politician to get the ear of the public by saying: If there is any money going the whites have got to have the first pickings, and if anything is left the "nigger" can have the leavings. This attitude of mind is deeply rooted and difficult to deal with. It creates inequalities which are far greater than those which stare one in the face, such as the rule that negroes must ride in separate compartments in trains and trams, which is not so terrible a grievance, provided that they get the same accommodation for the same money, as is generally the case.

The ruling elements in the governments of the South are now the professional classes among the whites, the lawyers and business men, and the small white farmers, who largely follow the lead of the former. The old governing class, the former slave-owning aristocracy, is politically and even socially extinct, for it is to be seen now only in a few seaside resorts, like Charleston, where the sons of former slave-owners live and dream of their past glories. The leadership of the conservative forces has passed into other hands. As in the Central European countries the old agrarian nobility has lost political power to the heads of industry and finance, combined with the impoverished middle classes and the small farmers. This is what has created Fascism in Italy and Hitlerism in Germany. The former slave areas of the United States are the one part of the continent in which I could see possibilities that a Fascist movement of the European type might develop. Democratic traditions are not quite so strong as in the North. There is a derelict agrarian nobility, industrial chiefs, and a class of poor and ignorant small white farmers. It is not an accident that Senator Huey Long has been able to found and lead a movement of his own in Louisiana.[1] Senator Bilbo leads a similar movement in Mississippi. Like European Fascists they aim ostensibly at big capital, but in effect their main attack is directed against the working class. It is a movement of small farmers and small shopkeepers. In Europe the Socialist and trade union section of the working class and the Jews bear the main brunt of the attack. In Long's Louisiana it is mainly the negro population that stands to lose. Just as in Germany it is easy to divert attention to the Jews, so here the negroes are in the same unhappy position.

But in spite of all these menacing features, it does appear that there has been considerable progress towards racial equality in the South. Lynchings are rare, now, and decreasing in number yearly, and for every one reported there are ten which are prevented and are not reported. The Inter-racial Commission gives a medal to every sheriff who stops a lynching. A typical comment on Southern politics, however, is the story told us in Atlanta of a sheriff who had stopped a lynching, and, when he was offered a medal, said that he would rather not have it, because he was going to stand for the State legislature at the next election, and did not want to appear before the white farmers as a protagonist of the negroes. Still, there has been progress, for some white trade unions are allowing negro workers to become members, and there is a tendency for the wages of the two races to approximate. Moreover, it is becoming more generally understood that the white population is in no danger of being swamped by the negroes. Indeed, the percentage of coloured people in the total population of the United States has steadily declined from 19·7 per cent in 1790 to 9 per cent in 1930. Though mixed marriages are forbidden in the Southern States, promiscuous relations are responsible for a large and increasing half-caste population, almost

[1] This was written before the assassination of Huey Long.

196

indistinguishable from the whites. Some authorities even think that in time the racial question will be solved in this way.

When my father was here in 1869 he saw the so-called Reconstruction Period which followed the Civil War, when the Southern slave-owners lay prostrate at the feet of the North, and when, after the assassination of Lincoln, there was no Northern statesman to hold out the hand of reconciliation. The so-called "carpet-baggers," or imported politicians, came in from the North, and with the aid of the military occupation disfranchised a large section of the whites and enfranchised the negroes, whose votes they proceeded to buy in order to humiliate the Southern whites. As my father said in his letters home, although the Southern whites richly deserved all they got, he was nevertheless, as a Liberal and a democrat, horrified to see what was being done in the name of Liberalism. The same old story may be seen throughout history. Moderate men start wars for ideals, with altrusitic aims, and extremists end these wars and make a peace which violates these ideals and denies these aims. So it was when Milton pleaded to Lord Protector Cromwell in the hour of his victory to beware of "hireling wolves" who would wreck his peace; so it was with the peace which ended the wars in Europe with the downfall of Louis XIV; so it was after the Great World War. And so it was in the case of the American Civil War. I know that there is a case which seeks to justify the action of the North in its dealings with the South after the war. I know that the South was offered better terms and an end of Reconstruction if they would accept negro suffrage, and that the people of the South refused, and still demanded the same number of seats in Congress, which would have given them representation out of proportion to their numbers. The Southern aristocracy needed a lesson apart from what they learned in the war, but surely not this lesson. Its fruits have been bitter indeed, and the North is much to blame for having excited, by its "Reconstruction" excesses, a reaction against the negroes as soon as the Northern military occupation ended. My father saw these excesses at their worst period. We, in 1934, saw the resultant reaction against the negroes. We saw the new dominating element among the Southern whites, the small white farmers, the business men, the professional classes and the "poor whites," blocking, as far as they could, the economic equality of the black race. But slowly the barriers are breaking down. I am not sure that the end of the reaction is not in sight.

In the afternoon of the day of our arrival in Atlanta we visited the Negro University there. Founded with the aid of the funds of the Northern Methodist Church and the Rockefeller Trust, it was created for the purpose of providing a college and even a university education for the negroes of the Southern States. Here we saw several hundreds of students preparing, with a fair academic equipment, for careers in the professions and in the sphere of administration. We met the Principal of the University, Dr. Hope, himself a negro, and the son of a former slave in Georgia. We lunched with him in the college dining-hall and afterwards met Professor Du Bois, a negro Professor of History. These men seem to have created an academic atmosphere in which their students can do good work. This can have been no easy task, in view of the racial prejudice existing all around them. To reflect that a generation ago these people were mainly slaves was to realize how far the negro race has progressed since then, and how much talent and ability are possessed by the race, even though these are still largely dormant. For this university provides, alas, only for a small minority, the intellectual cream of the negro race. And this has been made possible only by the money of

Northern millionaires, particularly the Rockefeller family, who cannot be too highly praised for what they have done in this respect, and also by the Northern Nonconformists— particularly the Baptists and Presbyterians. The Southern white Methodist churches, to their discredit, have done next to nothing to help, although the white Episcopal Church in North Carolina has been a notable and praiseworthy exception. It is sometimes said in extenuation of the educational policy of the Southern legislatures that the percentage of revenue spent on education is greater in the Southern than in the Northern states. I found on investigation that this only means that the population of the South, being agrarian in the main, and more scattered, have more spent on them per child because of the general higher cost of education in these areas. But the standard of education is definitely lower than in the North. When the Northern universities attempted to set standards of education most of the Southern educational institutions failed to reach these standards. Moreover, the greater part of the money allocated in the South for education goes to the white population, and only a very small percentage to the negroes. In the North, of course, the negro population is small, but the same amount is spent on it as on the white, and indeed the negroes attend the same schools.

On the following morning I was asked to attend the opening service of the day for the students in the large college hall. To my dismay I found that I was expected to say a few words to the students. Knowing how delicate the whole racial question is in the South I was by no means easy at the prospect. However, I told them that I was not there to pull the mote out of Uncle Sam's eye, when John Bull had a beam in his own (I was referring, of course, to the treatment of the negroes by the Union of South Africa). I went on to say that I thought the negroes had much to give to the culture of the American continent, especially in the sphere of art and music, and that if only the white man would grant them equality of opportunity in education, they should try to realize that this was one of the keys to the emancipation of their race. Later on they sang to us most beautifully. About a hundred young negro men, with deep bass voices, like a choir of Paul Robesons, sang negro spirituals. First came the negro National Hymn, "Lift every voice and sing." The students all fell naturally into taking their parts in harmony. They just became an impromptu choir. Then a glee quartet sang the old songs of the slave plantations, followed by some negro workmen's songs with a great deal of native humour in them. I suddenly realized that these people have a music, an outlook, and a sense of humour which are quite distinct from those of the other peoples of the American continent. These are not opposed to the white culture, as all wise Americans realize; they should be the means of enriching it. This was just what the Czech composer, Dvořák, felt when he came to America, and saw that the negroes were the only element in the population which had a native musical talent.

Finally, I noted a deep religious emotion running through the proceedings of that morning's opening ceremony. The negroes have learnt their religion from us whites. Unfortunately we have not told them that when a white man teaches a coloured man Christianity, he means that the commandment to "love one's neighbour as oneself" applies to the converted but not to the converter! Still, if there is one thing that I learnt from the Negro University at Atlanta it was that the negroes have intelligence enough to work out their own fate, given sufficient material support and moral sympathy. It would be a tragedy to try and mix the races in education. In the North they do so, because the negro population is so small. But the Yankee progressives would make a great mistake if, in their zeal for equality, they tried to co-educate the Southern whites alongside of Southern coloured people. The races should be kept separate in education, because only in this way can each develop on its own distinctive lines and contribute its quota to the common American culture. I fear that if they are mixed the coloured people will learn all the vices of the whites and none of their virtues, and that they will not develop their very valuable, if still dormant, qualities.

CHAPTER XI

THE HEART OF GEORGIA

From Atlanta we went on November 21st to Gainesville, a small country town about fifty miles to the north. Here we stayed with an American family with whom we had become acquainted by correspondence. Mr. and Mrs. Smith were members of an old Southern family, and several of their forebears had been slave-owners at the time of the Civil War. Mrs. Smith's uncle, to whom I shall refer later, had known my grandfather, had fought in the Civil War for the South, and had been wounded at the battle of Bull Run. From this family we had a typically warm American welcome, with the addition that it was also a Southern one. It is invidious to compare the Northerner and the Southerner in respect of the welcome they give us when we come from England. They are both equally friendly and hospitable. Only one real difference struck me. The Yankee wants to impress you with the United States as a whole. The Southerner wants you to love his Dixieland first and foremost, and after that you can admire the United States. My reactions to this were, that when I visited Northern homes I felt admiration for the whole people, for their open-heartedness, their freedom from snobbery and from standoffishness, and their readiness to tell you all you want to know about their country without any thought that you might have an ulterior motive. This candour and sincerity is one of the finest traits of the Americans, and is a complete contrast to the suspicion with which the traveller is regarded in the "police States" of Europe. Even in England we should not take the trouble to help foreigners with information about ourselves as the Americans do. This, I think, is probably due to our cold

exterior rather than to lack of good will. Once the outer
crust of reserve is broken down we can run a good second
to the Americans. Well, my reactions in Northern homes
was one of admiration for the people as a whole, as a brother
would admire a brother. But in a Southern home one felt
not admiration for the people, so much as love and emotion.
Sir Austen Chamberlain, when he was Foreign Secretary,
once said that one loved France as one loved a woman. I
felt the same affection for the South after coming into
contact with the Southern whites in their homes. One feels
as though one would like to modify all one's criticisms of
them in respect of their treatment of the negroes. It is hard to
be rational about the Southerners.

I soon found that the past is still very much alive in
Southern homes. I was unwise enough to mention at dinner
that my father had known and greatly respected General
Sherman. I suddenly recollected myself, and wished that
the earth would open and swallow me up, for I had said this
within fifty miles of the place where the famous march to the
sea began. But every Southerner has the manners of an
aristocrat, and knows how to get out of an awkward situation.
My *faux pas* was passed off by the general agreement that
Lincoln at any rate was a great man!

We listened with rapt attention to Mrs. Smith's stories,
which she had heard from her parents, of the Union troops
when they occupied the South. She spoke with as much
feeling as though the incidents related had happened yesterday. It seems that the turning loose of Yankee politicians
to plunder the aristocracy and run the South has been so
branded into the Southern soul that even the second
generation talks of it still. It must have made a terrible impression at the time. The Smiths had got a party together to
meet us, fairly representative of Gainesville. Mr. Smith himself, a member of a former slave-owning family, is engaged

203

in a successful insurance business. Then there was a well-known professor of history at the Gainesville Ladies' College, and thirdly, the manager of a textile business. When my father was here in 1869 the Southern aristocrats and local leaders of society were bemoaning their past glories, founded on slavery, and, like Narcissus, admiring their own reflection. But the second generation seemed to have pulled themselves together. The aristocratic South of my father's day has become absorbed into the professional and business class of the modern industrial State. But I heard of some Southerners who had retained their cotton plantations, and were working them with negro wage-labour in place of slave labour.

We heard all about the current politics of the day after dinner. Of course all present were ardent supporters of President Roosevelt and the Democratic Party, but this attitude was traditional. After meeting a party of Southerners in their home one realizes the heterogeneous nature of the majority which is behind the President in Congress. In New England I had found the Democrats mainly among the wage-earning working classes, apart from a sprinkling of professional men and women. In the Middle West the Democrats were farmers and ranchers. In California the people who supported Upton Sinclair were unskilled dock labourers, artisans and Spanish seasonal workers on the fruit plantations. In other words, the party division was to some extent on economic and occupational lines. But below the Mason-Dixon line everyone was a Democrat except the negro, and he didn't count. Governor Talmadge of Georgia who opposes the New Deal, the Tobacco magnates of North Carolina who like Trusts, the Liberal-minded small business men who dislike Trusts, the cotton planters who want cheap negro labour, the Labour leaders who want dear labour, the "poor white" farmers who want to "keep the nigger in his place," are all nominally Democrats and support the President.

The truth is that the South has not yet outlived the political traditions that arose out of the Civil War. Party organizations are still nominally aligned as though Sherman's troops had just marched out of the South, and the Democratic Party was still the bulwark of State rights against the oppressor in Washington. It is but dimly realized, and then only by a few, that if the New Deal is going to succeed it will have to increase rather than diminish the power of the Federal Government to interfere in the economic affairs of the States. As there is practically no Republican Party in the South, there are no elections, and there is no healthy competition between the two parties. The Democratic Party in the South is hardly a political party at all, but rather a private parliament in itself, engaged in sharing out administrative offices between the various classes of the community, and united on one main issue, the keeping of the negro in a subordinate position.

If the President desires to move to the Left in such matters as equality of public relief between the races, or the public ownership of electric power in the Appalachians, there will be no united party behind him in the South. This does not mean that the Democratic Party in the South will break up. In American politics the old parties exist less for advocating policies than for controlling local administration, and even the local judicial system, and hence far more latitude exists on questions of principle than can possibly exist in our English parties. Still, I was surprised to see how among those present that evening quite a number sympathized with the President in his policy of developing electrical power in the South as a public service, and so break the monopoly power of the Utility Corporations. Even on negro questions I found a more liberal outlook. One man told me that he had brought up some negroes, whom he knew and liked, to vote at a local election, had insisted on their voting, and had got his way.

Next day (November 22nd) we were taken to see an up-to-date textile mill which had been shifted South from New England, because, until recently, Southern labour was very cheap, and therefore very profitable. Now the President comes along with his Labour Codes, and what with a general ballyhoo and plenty of wireless talks he has public opinion on his side when he declares that it is not right to employ men for ten hours a day, and for half the pay they get in New England, when there are so many unemployed. So the Southern textile mills have had to mend their ways or be pilloried before the public, and we found that they had actually reduced working hours to eight and raised wages by 50 per cent. But the management had countered by putting in labour-saving machinery, so that no more men were employed than before, although those who were employed had better conditions. Thanks to the President, it seems that the industrial South is being made to lessen the disparity between it and the North in the treatment of labour and social conditions generally. Quite a lot of welfare work was being done in and round the textile factories: hospitals, cinemas, co-operative stores and playing fields. Until recently such things were unheard of in the South. But there was also a good deal of paternalism. The workers were not allowed to have vegetable gardens because they might spoil the appearance of the countryside. When I asked why they could not be given allotments away from their houses, I was naïvely told that the workers were generally too tired after they returned from work to be able to work in their gardens. This was the very opposite of what we had seen in Detroit at the Ford works.

Before we left Gainesville we looked round the little town.

It was like most American provincial towns, built of wood, with beautiful wide streets and fine avenues of trees. All these towns have the atmosphere of a garden city. Shoddy jerry-building, from which we suffer so greatly in England, does not obtrude itself here, although it does exist. Open spaces are so much greater that it is not noticed as it is in our little island. The houses were mostly of the one-storied colonial type, with a portico of Corinthian columns on the larger ones. The rooms are connected by folding doors. In the house of Mr. and Mrs. Smith we enjoyed a welcome relief from the overheating from which we had been suffering in the hotels and restaurants. I confess that the greatest discomfort which we ever had to endure in America was the dry heat of the houses. Americans have no idea how to regulate their heat. I found in October furnaces heated up as they would be in January. I am sure that American women would enhance their attractiveness, already very great, if they lived in a house atmosphere which did not spoil their complexions. The famous complexions of our English women are partly due to our reasonably cool and freely ventilated houses. Of course, climatic conditions in the two countries are very different, and Americans coming to England complain that we freeze them.

In the centre of the square at Gainesville was a typical monument: a Confederate soldier gazing pensively towards the "deep South" with its pine-clad flats, its forests and cotton plantations. Beneath it were engraven the words: "To Our Glorious Confederate Dead," entwined round the emblem of the Stars and Bars. This monument had not been erected so very long. The South is still in such a mood that when a town has sufficient money to spend, it erects a statue to commemorate a war that took place seventy years ago. The South thinks still of this war—not of the recent Great World War. Yet I heard that the Southern emblem of

the Stars and Bars has been seen in the streets of Washington.
Feeling has calmed down sufficiently for the Daughters of
the Confederacy to attend conferences in the Federal
Capital and to show their flag side by side with the Stars and
Stripes without the Northerners taking offence. The wounds
that the sister States inflicted on each other over half a
century ago are slowly healing.

I must not forget to mention the negro quarters at Gainesville. One stumbles upon them, as it were, by accident. It is
here that the servant-girls employed in the white houses
return home after dark. They are pathetic little Uncle Tom's
Cabins, away from the main streets, away from street lighting
and all the modern conveniences of a town. The roads are
unpaved and full of ruts, and everything indicates poor
wages and under-employment. I heard that the landlords
are whites, that no street paving is undertaken without their
consent, and they are not interested in improvements.
Most pathetic of all were the Christian churches of the
negroes: little wooden barns with tiny, rickety crosses on
them, suggesting that they were hoping to make up in the
next world what has been denied them in this.

On November 22nd we travelled to Savannah from Atlanta
by the "Central of Georgia." The railway followed to a large
extent the line of General Sherman's famous march to the
sea. Looking out from the train one could see flat country
all the way, and swamps interspersed with pine forests.
Along most of the route were cotton plantations, both small
and large holdings. They were formerly worked by slaves,
but now there are dismal little villages of negroes dotted
about. These negroes were trying to earn a living by working
the plantations without capital, depending on credit from
the local store manager. One could picture Sherman's
dashing Yankee boys marching "from Atlanta to the sea,"
and "the darkies shouting when they heard the joyful sound."

But I saw nothing joyful about either the darkie or the white share-cropper with cotton at 6 cents the pound, as it has been for the last three years. Now it is a little dearer they may just be able to pay some of their debts. Their slavery has been transferred from the aristocrat to the local usurer.

Arrived at Savannah we went at once to see Mrs. Caroline Wilson. I had known this lady by correspondence for many years. She is the daughter of Colonel William Pearce Price, who was Member of Congress for Georgia at the end of the Reconstruction Period, when my grandfather, William Philip Price, was member of the British House of Commons for Gloucester. Because of their identical initials and name they seem to have got in touch with each other. They were interested to discover a common ancestry by research into Welsh pedigrees. Remote ancestors in both cases were traced back to Breconshire, but the connection is difficult to prove, since Welsh family names were not fixed before the eighteenth century. William Pearce Price's father was a slave-owner, but the son became a lawyer and practised in the provinces. He fought in the Civil War for the South, and after the withdrawal of the Union troops was elected for Congress. I found Mrs. Wilson a most typical and charming representative of an old cultured Southern family, which had not allowed adversity, when the Confederacy collapsed, to overwhelm it, but had at once realized the need for the South to strike out along a new line. Her daughters were all married to enterprising business men, some of them working in the North. She had a grandson in the American Navy, and two of her daughters were not too proud to run a tasteful art shop in Savannah. This is typical of the way in which the best elements of the Southern aristocracy met the new situation following the war between the States.

Mrs. Wilson had a fund of stories and reminiscences of

o

American life in the old days. Like many others of her *milieu*, she could talk of the war as if it had happened yesterday. In spite of advanced years she was amazingly alert, and was busy compiling a history of the colonial families of old Georgia. She took us round in a car, with two of her daughters, to see Savannah, an old colonial town, founded in the reign of George II. The younger sons of the country gentry of Southern England had come here to seek their fortunes by growing cotton and tobacco with African slave labour. What a different type from the settlers in New England, who left England because they had to do so, if they were to have freedom of religious worship, and then became the sturdy independent farmers and business men who are the backbone of Yankee America to-day! This one fact is enough to explain the calamity of the war between the States.

Savannah, with its houses and its sub-tropical vegetation, was rather like a French watering-place, though beneath the surface one could see its commercial activities. Savannah River broadens out into a harbour where British ships were waiting to load up with cotton for Lancashire. We visited the British Consul and other prominent local persons. The heat was great and the air sultry. I found it hard to talk about the price of cotton and the New Deal, and so did most of the people I met. I could see why people in Dixieland are contemplative rather than active, and prefer the amenities of life to mere money-grubbing. The private houses which we entered seemed all organized for comfort. I saw some good collections of books, and books too which appeared to be read, and delightful easy-chairs; and most houses that did not front on to the main streets had gardens where one could lie in hammocks under the palms and gaze on the magnolias in bloom, while negro servants brought refreshing drinks. How could anyone want to leave this land and go pioneering in California and the Rockies? Leave that to the Yankees! I felt just the same myself. Where we were staying there was a swimming-bath, and although it was the end of November I soon found myself bathing and basking in the sunshine, while green bananas hung down from the leafy shade above my head.

Later in the day Mrs. Wilson's daughters took us to see an old slave plantation about five miles out of the town— the old Hermitage. It is derelict and half a ruin. Passing through fields of corn and cotton at the edge of the negro quarter of Savannah, we approached a long avenue of evergreen oaks. At the end of it was an empty house in Georgian style, where the former slave-owner used to live. The walls and roof were good, but the floors had fallen in. We could see the different rooms where the slave-owning family had lived, and where the master interviewed the overseer. There was the old garden, overgrown with weeds, the wine-cellar, the overseer's house, and close by were long rows of tiny little brick houses about 12 to 15 feet square. In these hovels the slaves lived and reared their families. In actual fact they only slept there, for they were fed in a large eating-house, and the children had a common play-room. Then there were the storehouses and the rice-mill, and the place where the slaves were bought and sold by auction. We wandered about the place, and pictured all the scenes that might have taken place there. I suppose it must have been a quiet and peaceful life, and the slaves were probably better treated and looked after than their so-called free descendants are today, up to their neck in debt as share-croppers to the local usurer. We saw the spot where Sherman's troops—commanded by the same Sherman who had taken my father and mother through New Mexico— had shot deserters from the Union army and so-called spies of the Confederates. When our two lady companions described this tragic incident we could feel their deep emotion; it was as though the harsh deed had been committed only yesterday. We could only listen in sympathetic silence, and then point to the spot where the human slaves were bought and sold.[1]

Late that evening I strolled down to the quayside at Savannah. There I saw a row of thin and ragged negroes fishing with hook and line. What they might catch was all they would eat that day. They were dull and listless, human derelicts, some of them former share-croppers who had lost their all. No public relief for them! No fairy godmother from Washington had brought them anything. The Georgian legislature which dispenses Federal relief funds had no thought for them. Yet when I talked to them, they brightened up; one of them began to sing and another to laugh. The negro is never resentful, even when suffering most. He is saved by his sense of humour and his musical soul.

[1] Since writing the above I hear that the old Savannah Hermitage has been bought by Henry Ford, and will be taken down and rebuilt in Bryans County, Georgia, in an appropriate spot, as a lasting memorial of a Southern slave plantation.

CHAPTER XII

THE TWO CAROLINAS—OLD SOUTH
AND NEW

I HAD not been long in the South before I began to long for a little Northern efficiency. Travelling in these parts reminded me a little of travelling in Ireland or Russia. There was always a glorious uncertainty about everything. Negro porters at the hotel tell you that the train goes at such and such an hour. The railway porters will tell you another time. You ask for tea and toast in your hotel, and you get grape-fruit and eggs. But it is all done with such smiling good nature that you cannot possibly be cross. In actual fact, thanks to a muddle over trains, we conceived the idea of traversing a part of South Carolina by bus and visiting Charleston, so I had no real grounds for blaming the incompetence of my informers.

The road northwards from Savannah runs about fifty miles inland from the coast, passing through flat country, large parts of which are water-logged and overgrown with Swamp Cypress, and there are drier tracts of Loblolly and Long-leaved Pine forest. Other tracts are derelict. Once upon a time rice was grown in abundance here with the aid of slave labour. But with the end of slavery and the coming of cheap rice from the Far East this form of rural economy collapsed.

In this flat country we saw numerous clearings in the forest, where negro and poor white settlers were working cotton and corn plots. The negroes were the descendants of slaves who settled on this miserable land after they had got their "freedom."

The "poor whites" had always been there. They were the

descendants of the original white colonists who had never had the good fortune to become the owners of slaves. Consequently they were without capital to work their land, and they could not hire themselves out for wages because slave labour everywhere undermined their position. They could not work on the plantations, for no slave-owner wanted wage labour; they could not become artisans, or small tradesmen, because here too the slaves would have been their competitors. We thought when we saw a play in New York called *Tobacco Road*, that this was a gross caricature of the state of affairs in the South, but our journey through South Carolina convinced us that it was rather an understatement.

The position of the poor white is possibly even worse than that of the negro, for he is despised both by the coloured people and by the wealthier whites. I realized for the first time that the number of whites who benefited by slavery was extraordinarily small. Yet the "poor whites" all flocked to the Stars and Bars to defend slavery in the war, although its existence had been the cause of their own ruin. What a fine example of the truth that human actions are governed by irrational impulse rather than by logic!

We had long stops between buses at various places on our way to Charleston, our destination. We stopped at small towns or large villages, where there was generally a post-office, a police station, and a store. Wooden houses of colonial type lay on either side of a deeply-rutted sandy road. Unemployed and ragged negroes were hanging about. Some white cadets from the naval training ship at Charleston were marching along the street. Insulting remarks were hurled at the negroes, who cowered and slunk away out of sight. A negro girl crossed the road; I heard lewd remarks bawled across to her by some whites outside a shop. About a mile down the road was a batch of wooden huts, precariously resting on stones at the four corners. The wood was hand-sawn and there was only one room in each hut. The inmates were generally a negro man and woman. There were children of various ages. The man was the only member of the family who had proper clothes. The rest were half naked. The food, I gathered, consisted of hand-ground maize meal, baked into flat cakes. I did not see that there was anything else, except what the local store would advance on security of the cotton crop. If it failed there would be nothing but what could be obtained by begging from the passengers who got off the buses at the halt up the road. I looked at the fields, where the hope of future food lay. The cotton-field was half covered with weeds, and there were no implements for cultivation, save such as the storekeeper would lend them, repaying himself out of the price of the food which he would sell them in the winter. This food was sold only on credit. The maize-cobs had been gathered but half the crop was weeds, as I could see from what remained on the field. I walked back up the road firm in the conviction that the conditions of the peasants in Russia under the Tsar, as I had seen them, were greatly superior to those of the negro share-cropper and the "poor white" in South Carolina! The Tsarist Government did permit a certain amount of co-operation and self-help, which the peasants organized among themselves. There was a society and a local public opinion which could express itself in village meetings, as long as it did not speak against the Government. But here there was nothing. Everyone was free to say anything he liked and to starve. Here an old economy, based on slavery, had collapsed, and nothing had taken its place. The human wreckage released by the collapse had been allowed to drift aimlessly about for sixty years. Society had simply decayed and died here. There was in fact no society or social consciousness whatever. I remembered that Southern whites had told me from time to time that the South really understands the negro and loves him, and that only in the South is the negro really at home. That may be so, but even a dog likes his kennel, because he knows nothing else. Somehow I prefer the Yankee's attitude. He says openly that he does not like the negroes, but that they are, nevertheless, entitled to a square deal and equal rights of citizenship under the Constitution.

Arrived at Charleston we went round the town. We were much impressed by this most perfect of all the old English colonial settlements of America. Founded in the reign of Charles II the English colonists, mostly the sons of well-to-do families, brought English customs, and even English materials for building their houses. I saw several houses of the Queen Anne style which one might see in any South of England village today. It was only the palms growing in the streets, the absence of the English elm and oak, which prevented one from imagining that one was in Bournemouth or some Devonshire seaside resort. From the fine sea-front the Atlantic Ocean was visible through a wide channel, in which stood the famous Fort Sumpter, where the first shot in the war between the States was fired.

Here in Charleston one can still see what is left of the real old Southern aristocracy, or at least those of its members who have any money left. In the main, however, the fine villas along the sea-front are occupied during the winter season by Northern business people from New York and Chicago. The slump has reduced their numbers somewhat, but the process of penetrating the Old South by new blood from the North is still continuing.

The monuments of the Old South are still visible everywhere. Foremost among them is the statue and house of John C. Calhoun, that grim figure and eloquent warrior of dying causes. In the City Hall the walls were hung with portraits of Confederate leaders, whose memory still lives in Charleston. But the life of this fine old City of the South is being slowly drawn into the main stream of American life, both economic and cultural. Chain stores, Woolworths, overland bus services and wireless are breaking down the barriers of particularism which have held South Carolina apart from the rest of the United States. Nevertheless I think this Old South will continue to contribute something to the life of the new America. I was shown with pride by a Charlestonian those words on the grave in St. Michaels Church of James Louis Petigru, jurist, statesman and orator of South Carolina, who died in 1863; "Unawed by Opinion, Unseduced by Flattery, Undismayed by Disaster, He confronted Life with Antique Courage and Death with Christian Hope." These words were much appreciated by the late President Woodrow Wilson.

After our motor-drive through South Carolina we caught the night express northwards and found ourselves landed next morning at a little wayside junction deep in the heart of North Carolina. We were anxious to round off our impressions of Dixieland in this the State that was supposed to be the most progressive and the most closely in touch with the North. My first impression may have been a superficial one, but I thought it important at the time. The little branch-line train that was to carry us to the town of Durham consisted of two coaches. The engine was driven and fired by two negroes in the full cotton overall uniform of the qualified American mechanic. Even the peaked forage-cap was there. Now I had not seen this anywhere in either Georgia or South Carolina. Evidently the white railway workers have not raised any objection to working in the same grades and on the same line as the negro workers. Arrived at Durham we found the station full of negroes who had come into town for market-day. In the streets there was an atmosphere of bustle and hurry that struck us forcibly, for we had not encountered it since we had been in the South. I saw no dejected negroes hanging about the streets. They all seemed as busy as the white Americans. There were plenty of negro shops, and everybody was dressed reasonably well and tidily. Indeed, I soon learned that this town supports a negro millionaire, who is the head of a prosperous insurance business. There was a good deal of industry in the town too, mostly connected with tobacco and cigarette manufacture. We saw Durham University, which was founded and financed by influential people in the tobacco industry. But of late years the tobacco interests have extended their influence into electric power, and have been behind some of the utility corporations which have come into such disfavour with the President and the public because of their high charges. These tobacco-power interests have been working very hard against the President's Tennessee Power Scheme, and their methods have not stopped short of trying to mobilize the services of the professors and college authorities, whom they can control through the power of the purse. The latter were expected to go to Washington and lobby in Congress against the President's Tennessee Power Scheme. From other sources I learnt that these interests were not averse to exploiting the negro also, and exciting race prejudice against the employment of white labour on the Power Scheme. I confess I was not favourably impressed by the position of certain American universities. While financial influences in England are not against lobbying in their interests, and exert an appalling control over the Press, they stop short of trying to control the universities and colleges. From what I could learn it seemed that public opinion in America was hardening against this sort of thing. I heard some very candid remarks during my stay here, and later in Washington.

In the next place that we visited we saw a model type of educational institution. About twenty miles to the south after motoring through undulating woodlands and cornfields, interspersed with large built-up areas, we reached the beautiful little university town of Chapel Hill. The town seemed to have been carefully planned, with wide streets and spacious gardens and parks. It is always a pleasing feature of American towns that the gardens of one house run into the gardens of another, without a hedge or even a fence, such as one would see in England. This seems to indicate the greater sociability of the Americans. It is in keeping too with the lack of snobbishness to which I have referred elsewhere. This was particularly noticeable in Chapel Hill. The houses were mostly of the wooden colonial type, and the University buildings were fine brick imitations of European eighteenth-century architecture. A graceful clock tower rose above the rest, and every evening a carillon of bells, played by students, resounded over the gently undulating forests and fields that stretched away to the horizon on every side. If the physical aspect of Chapel Hill was pleasing, the intellectual aspect of its university was equally so. Being under the State of North Carolina its work was not hindered by the political views of trust magnates. Through Mrs. Lyman Cotton, one of the librarians of the University, to whom we had introductions, we saw something of the educational work being done here. At a dinner-party at Mrs. Cotton's we met a representative group of leaders of thought at Chapel Hill, and next day (November 25th) we lunched with Professor Graham, the Principal of the University. We were immediately struck by the attitude towards the negro, very different from that which we had noticed in Georgia and South Carolina. Here there was a feeling of anxiety about the condition of the negro, and a desire to educate him, so that he could appreciate the full responsibilities of citizenship. There was not that patronizing declaration of love for the negro, coupled with a supreme indifference to his economic and spiritual welfare, which we had noted further south. The Chapel Hill University was clearly creating a liberal outlook on the race question, and on all problems, social and economic, was cultivating an inquiring and sympathetic approach. I felt that while an American form of Fascism or Communism might develop at any time in the more southerly States, such a development would be impossible in North Carolina, if Chapel Hill was at all typical of its outlook. The general atmosphere was like that evoked by reading the *Manchester Guardian*, or talking with progressive thinkers at Oxford or Cambridge. The students were being taught by the creation of a mental state rather than by the assertion of dogma that sympathy with the less fortunate was necessary, and that the method of democratic and open discussion is the way to achievement.

On our first afternoon in Chapel Hill I received another striking impression. I witnessed a football match between two negro teams, which the white students at the University attended in considerable numbers, and cheered enthusiastically. On the following day we attended a concert given by negro singers, the proceeds of which were in aid of a negro college in a neighbouring town. The chairman at the concert was none other than Professor Graham and more than half the audience were whites.

On the second afternoon I went for a long walk into the country round Chapel Hill. Beyond the villas and the homes of those working in the town I came upon little farms of cotton and corn. I chatted with an old negro to whom one of these holdings belonged. I could see at once that this was a very different type of holding to those I had seen in the tragic countryside of South Carolina. There was no dependence here on a single cash crop which was mortgaged to a local tradesman. There was stock on this holding. In a couple of rough sheds were some cows, and in the stubble-field bordering the forest a herd of pigs was roaming. There was also some poultry about the place. The farmer must have either inherited some capital or been loaned money at reasonable rates to enable him to run a holding of this kind. The result was that he was independent and able to look his fellow-man in the face—as he looked in mine, in his kindly, smiling negro fashion. But stripped of his negro-American accent and phrases, what he told me was simply what the Middle Western farmers had said and what our British farmers say also: namely, that prices are too low, though they have been a little better lately, and the costs of running a farm too high. Then we fell to talking about manures and animal diseases. Further on were some small white farmers. I did not get into talk with them, but their holdings seemed to me of the same type as those of the negro farmer. Socially these two types of people were not on the same level. The colour bar still prevailed. But economically they were equals, and that is the thing that matters in these days.

Next day happened to be Sunday, so we went to a negro chapel to hear one of the services. It was a very interesting experience. The people worked themselves into a frenzy of religious emotion, and shouted and moaned aloud. One old negro who "led in prayer" uplifted his voice in a crescendo, and finally his whole body shook as his words became more and more incoherent. The preacher told us there were only two ways to go; one was to Heaven and the other to Damnation. He spoke as if he really believed in an anthropomorphic God, and as though angels might appear at any time and carry him off to Heaven. And I believe the congregation believed this literally too. At times, when I heard them praying, with their voices rising and falling, I seemed to hear the primitive tribes of the jungle performing their rites before their idols. At other times the sound was such as I had often heard in Central Asia, when the Tartar tribes said their noontide prayers. They were very nice to us, the only white people at the service, and at the close the preacher asked me if I would like to say something. I uttered a few platitudes about understanding between the white and black races and then summoned up courage to say that as well as believing in God, they ought to believe in themselves and educate themselves, a sentiment which they applauded, but I doubt if they understood how to set about it. I think there can be no doubt that the lack of clear reasoning power has caused these coloured races to give way to religious emotion as the only outlet for their spiritual energy. We whites have taught them a form of Evangelical Protestantism, to understand which requires a certain standard of reasoning and power of discrimination and logic. Having taught them the forms of this religion we have entirely omitted to educate them to use their brains and enjoy it. The natural result is that their interpretation of it runs into all sorts of emotional excess. A rational religion has been bestowed upon an emotional people without any intellectual preparation, with the result that they go into hysterics as they pray, and the perspiration streams from their faces. It would have been better, failing proper education, if they had been given Roman Catholicism, Greek Orthodoxy or Armenian Gregorianism to digest than that they should have been converted to Evangelical Protestantism without being able to understand it. I understand, however, that this phenomenon is not confined to the negroes, and that in the mountains of North and South Carolina tucked away in the backwoods, are ancient settlements of "poor whites" who practise their Evangelicalism in just the same way. There is even a sect of "Holy Rollers" who roll upon the ground in ecstasy. This only proves again that this is the natural effect of a crudely-taught religion upon very poor people of all colours who have never been trained to think. The following day I met the Episcopal Bishop of North Carolina at Raleigh, and I found that he held very strongly that the task of the white churches in the South is just this task of teaching the negro to interpret his Protestantism as the majority of his white brothers do.

Our last stop in North Carolina was at Raleigh, the capital of the State, which we reached by car on the morning of November 26th. It had been arranged that I should meet the Governor, Mr. Eringhaus, at the Capitol. Mr. Eringhaus received me in his room at the Capitol, and our conversation covered a wide range of subjects. What struck me most in this interview was that for the first half of the time that I was with him it was he who asked me questions about England. We had been struck on several occasions during our travels by the great interest which Americans seemed to be taking in the affairs of Europe, and particularly in British social legislation. I found Governor Eringhaus especially interested in learning how we worked our unemployment insurance system and our public relief, and what legislation we had for the control of trade-union activity. After a time I had to remind him that I was as interested in learning about the United States as he was in learning about England. So our interview resulted in an exchange of views about our respective countries which was useful to both of us. I confess that I was flattered to feel that the old country's experience in social welfare work should arouse such interest in the United States. But of one thing I am certain: it is impossible and indeed hardly desirable that the States should copy England. The size and complexity of the United States, and the difficulty of central government, is so great that other methods will be necessary. England is small, compact and relatively centralized. Still, America can apply some of our experience to her own conditions, for England is undoubtedly ahead of the United States in social legislation, just as the latter is ahead in efficient industrial organization, and mass-production technique, and in every sort of useful device for making life easier.

From the Governor I went to the Raleigh Agricultural Research Department of the State University. Here I found an admirable body of intelligent workers engaged in studying the agricultural problem of North Carolina in all its aspects, including the social. The facts which they placed before me confirmed what I had long suspected, that the colour question in the South is really not so acute as the economic question is becoming. Thus in the whole of the South there is an enormous "poor white" population which gets its living from the land, while there is an appreciable negro population which owns land or consists of independent tenant farmers with capital. The figures are:

	White	Coloured
Landowners . .	1,200,000	200,000
Tenant Farmers .	700,000	300,000
Poor Share-croppers	400,000	400,000
	2,300,000	900,000

This shows that the share-cropper problem affects in an equal degree the white and the coloured population. Between 1920 and 1929 in North Carolina half a million people, both white and coloured, left the land and sought employment in the towns and cities. The industrial depression has stopped this outlet, and the annual surplus of the rural population is frozen into the rural areas. This surplus population roughly is half white and half coloured. The proof that it is accumulating can be seen in the fact that, although farm incomes have been rising since the Agricultural Adjustment Act, there has been a steady increase throughout North

Carolina in the amount of money which has had to be paid to the rural areas for the relief of destitution. Altogether, throughout the whole of the South, 239,572,187 dollars has been distributed during 1934 to cotton-growers under the scheme to control cotton acreage. But there can be little doubt that the greater part of this has gone to the large plantation owners, and the money lenders and creditors who finance the share-croppers. Meanwhile the population in the villages living on charity increases. These people are recruited partly from share-croppers who have got so deeply into debt that they have been unable to carry on, and partly from the natural increase in population which under the land-tenure system cannot get started on the land.

The agricultural experts in North Carolina are of opinion that until there is a reform in the system of land tenure the problem of poverty in the rural areas will become more acute, and may even reach the stage of catastrophe. The liberation of the share-croppers from the clutches of usury, the setting up of schemes of public credit to aid the small cultivators, and finally a plan to settle them on the land, either as State tenants or as peasant proprietors, as was done under the Wyndham Act in Ireland, are all possible avenues along which solutions may be found. That indeed appears to be the most urgent problem in the South, which in land tenure and in general social welfare is fifty years behind the rest of the United States. But at least I had the impression that in North Carolina there were plenty of people who were aware of this problem, and were anxious to do something about it. In Georgia and South Carolina I found no one who even seemed to realize the existence of the problem.

CHAPTER XIII

THE FEDERAL CAPITAL

IT was altogether fitting that we should end our trek across
the continent with five days in Washington. Here we arrived
on November 27th, to crown our final impressions of this
country with a sight of its Federal heart. It seems that one
day Washington is going to be one of the most imposing
capitals in the world. In spaciousness, grandeur and wise
planning it is already unsurpassed, though one sees it as yet
only half completed. If Constantinople has ancient history
and Oriental glamour to embellish it, Washington has
modern history written on its face, and has concentrated
in it and around it the symbols of a century and a half
of America's past in impressive monuments, parks and
buildings.

We saw the memorials of three momentous phases of
American history in Washington. The first of these we saw
on the pilgrimage which we made to Mount Vernon. This
is the conventional thing to do; nevertheless, it should be
done, because only there can one visualize the Fathers of
the American Republic and its constitution, the kind of men
they were and the life they led. When one looks on the
quiet countryside through which the Potomac flows, and
sees the former homes of the early American country
squires with their stables and fox-hunting kennels, their
libraries for cultured leisure, their gardens and home farms,
one realizes how these men were transplanting eighteenth-
century England into the New World. But one sees also that
they refused to transplant eighteenth-century political ideas
of aristocratic Europe in the new land of opportunity,
where rewards awaited energy and enterprise. So the

peaceful Conservative fox-hunting country squire was made a rebel, and a successful rebel too, and I always think we British must thank him and his colleagues for having, together with our Whigs, like Burke and Fox, exposed the unhealthy side of eighteenth-century British public life, and so eased our passage into the middle-class democracy of the nineteenth century. The shock which our Tory country squires got from the New World helped to discredit them and all they stood for. It was fitting that on our first day in Washington we should visit Mount Vernon, and in the evening see at the theatre that fine play, *Valley Forge*.

On the following day we saw the symbol of the second momentous phase of American history, the Lincoln Memorial. I saw no building on American soil that so completely overwhelmed us with its simple dignity and its majesty. In that quiet park, dotted with ponds and shrubs, we entered through the great columns, stood before the statue of Abraham Lincoln, and engraved on the walls read the immortal words from his Second Inaugural Address and his speech at Gettysburg. This stately building immortalizes for posterity the titanic struggle which convulsed the Northern continent. I felt as I stood there that it was not slavery alone that caused that convulsion, but that the question was here decided whether the United States was to travel along the road of a modern State, and unify the thought and culture of the whole country to the north of the Gulf of Mexico, or whether it was to sink into the insignificance of small, loosely confederated States, the prey of the intrigues of European oligarchs and despots. Was this land to become a real United States or the Balkan States of North America?

And then came the third momentous phase of American history of which we were to see the monuments on our third day; the grave of the Unknown Soldier in the Great

227

War, and the War Memorial building. In the same category I would place also the tomb of President Woodrow Wilson in the unfinished Episcopal Cathedral. At both of these one realizes what a colossal break the events, which these memorials symbolize, had caused in the course of American history. The United States had come out of her continent and had played a part in the affairs of Europe; had assumed, in fact, the responsibilities of a Great World Power. This would have caused the Constitution Fathers to turn in their graves, and even Abraham Lincoln's great mind could hardly have visualized this development, when he struggled for the unity of the continent. And yet the grave of the Unknown Soldier was the natural sequence to the Lincoln Memorial, as perhaps the premature grave of President Wilson was a sequel to the Great War. As I stood before that tomb, I realized the tragedy of that sincere, dogmatic mind. He seems to have caught a glimpse of the phase beyond the Great War. The United States had taken part in a world struggle, and had gone outside its continent. Was it merely to return when all was over, or was it to help to build up a new structure of public law and international justice? For a moment that vision shone, and then was blotted out. The politicians of the Senate saw to that. The great reaction to traditional American policy had taken place.

I found myself asking while I was in Washington: Where had I seen during our journey any outward sign of hostility to the idea that the United States should more directly participate in world affairs? Towards Britain I had observed nothing but the greatest friendliness, which I believed to be of the sincerest kind. Towards Europe and even towards the League of Nations I had found no vestige of hostility, but only a feeling of doubt and caution. The Administration had given evidence some time ago of its desire to help the League by a declaration of American neutrality in the event

228

of the League's conflict with an aggressor under the covenant provided that steps were taken towards general disarmament. Everything seemed to be moving a few years ago back to the direction for which Wilson had worked. And yet I had an uneasy feeling that today there was something hidden from me, which was still holding the United States in its traditional policy of isolation. The liberal intellectuals of New England have long been opposed to that traditional policy. But even in the Middle West, where I expected to find isolationism, I heard nothing in its favour. The Irish population seemed to me, where I had met it, to be, as it always has been, a disturbing element. It is the only anti-British element left in the United States, but it is not fighting in the open now. I think, however, that the Irish element, through its hold on the Tammany organizations all over the country, exerts an influence for the traditional policy of American isolation. Doubtless it fears instinctively that new ideas may bring new types of politicians, and thus become a threat to its organizations. Amongst business people I had noted a growing realization that the United States is economically part of a world system. It is common talk everywhere that the American tariffs are too high, and are helping to kill world trade: that the United States cannot retain its standard of living unless it recovers some of its lost international trade. What then is hindering its more active participation in the work of the League of Nations and the International Court of Arbitration?

On thinking it over I could only come to the conclusion that there are probably a number of causes. Firstly, the people of the United States are so immersed in their own immediate internal problems, such as Labour Codes, relief, and public works, Stock-Exchange reform, public utilities, the negro question, Federal and State rights, &c., that the public mind cannot easily concentrate on international questions. Secondly, the hope is still there, though not often expressed openly, that the country can pull through by relying on its own resources, and, if necessary, by becoming more self-sufficient than it is at present. Public opinion is probably in advance of Congress and the Senate, but it is not active enough, and owing to a certain lack of will-power and direction the old traditional foreign policies tend to prevail. Politicians interested in no change and radio-priests can always attract attention and tip the evenly-balanced scales of public opinion by raising the conventional cry: "No foreign entanglements."

Undoubtedly, also, the steady worsening of the European situation during the last three years has not improved matters. The failure of the Disarmament Conference, the tacit support of Japan in Manchuria by Sir John Simon, the withdrawal of Germany from the League, and the rearming of Germany, have created a feeling that at least the United States of America must keep out of the Hell's kitchen this time. Since I left the United States of America, the feeling of doubt about the League and Europe has crystallized into fear, and the determination not to be involved again. Hence a systematic search for legislation to keep the country neutral in war at all costs, and free from foreign entanglements. But there is this difference from the old attitude: Neutrality now means not the right to trade with a belligerent and break a blockade. It means a refusal to trade with *any* belligerent, a pacific withdrawal of the United States of America into its own shell. This at least will leave the League free from the fear of complications with the United States of America, when trying to organize sanctions to restrain an aggressor under the Covenant. America's sense of world responsibility, growing but still timorous, together with her terror of being embroiled in another war, has forced her willy-nilly into an attitude of benevolent neutrality towards the

League. This is a factor today of supreme importance to world law and order.

We had no opportunity of seeing the Federal politicians at work, for Congress was not sitting, and the President was away taking the waters. However, we had an interview with Mr. Wallace, the Secretary of Agriculture, and with Mr. Ickes, the Secretary for the Interior. We saw a good deal of the Department of Agriculture, that colossal building which has become such a hive of industry in the attempt of the Roosevelt Administration to rescue American agriculture from ruin. One is impressed both here and in the other Federal departments with the existence of an efficient civil service, the complete absence of which is such a feature of the public administration of the States and the municipalities. The spoils system has ruined local government but in Washington a tradition of public service is being built up and a body of men is being created which has all the drive and efficiency which has hitherto been the monopoly only of big business and private enterprise. The growing public conscience of the United States will soon have an adequate body of public servants to minister to its wants.

In certain rooms in the Department of Agriculture I saw maps hung on the wall. Every State of the Union was depicted on these maps, and in each State coloured flags marked the spots where derelict farm colonies had been left stranded since the slump. Some of these I had seen in the Middle West. Washington apparently has a plan for these. The chaotic method of settlement which operated hitherto was to be replaced by planning. There are still unsettled tracts where a living can be made out West. Surveys have shown that they have been neglected by the speculator. But what, I asked, if these new settlements begin to produce corn, hogs, and wheat, and upset the crop-planning with its processing taxes? The idea is, I was told, that these shall be subsistence farms. It will be difficult to make them self-supporting, but it is hoped that subsidiary employment will be found in State or Federal forests, rural industries, national parks, and public utilities. It is the essence of the same problem that we have in England with our frozen-in, redundant industrial population in certain areas. We too have our plans for subsistence holdings with alternative employment. But we have fewer opportunities than the United States, with its huge forest resources and endless possibilities of developing national parks. That, then, is one line of policy that the Department of Agriculture is working on—re-settlement on the land on subsistence farms; and this carries with it the necessity to restrict the output of agricultural produce in the absence of any chance of re-establishing the sale of American wheat and meat products abroad.

There are those in the Department who are examining this aspect of the problem. They realize that Europe will take no more of this produce unless it is paid for by industrial imports from Europe. They contend, however, that the natural flow of trade between Great Britain and the United States is triangular and proceeds *via* South America. Can Great Britain export manufactured goods again to Brazil and the Argentine, who in turn will export tropical products to the States, who in their turn will send northern products to Great Britain? The delicate strands of this once automatic exchange have been torn to shreds by the convulsions of recent years. It requires a strong optimist to expect its re-establishment. Failing that, however, the United States seems destined to follow the line of least resistance, as other countries are doing, and to live more within itself, planning its production and placing its surplus population on subsistence farms. But that will mean a permanently lower standard of living, and I don't think this is generally realized.

But at least in Washington one could see that the Roosevelt Administration, within the framework of national self-sufficiency, was trying to lead public opinion. Over a large part of the Union people have become aware that the old frontiers of buffaloes and Indians have gone, and that new frontiers of social responsibilities to their fellow citizens are springing up. And President Roosevelt has become the national embodiment of that feeling. The November elections of 1934 showed that the mass of public opinion among the working classes, the middle classes, and the professional and farming classes supported the New Deal from the Atlantic to the Pacific. But is the backing of a majority of public opinion as expressed in Congress sufficient to enable a President to carry through great legislative changes? One has reasons for grave doubt. The American Constitution is the greatest obstacle to social and economic change that has ever been forged by constitutional lawyers. We in England are apt to think of the United States of America in terms of our own constitution. We think that if a Congress is elected by popular vote it can go forward like an English Parliament, and carry out its mandate, even if this means using a Parliament Act to overcome an Upper House. But the United States of America Congress has a much more dangerous obstacle than a House of Lords to overcome, and it has no Parliament Act with which to defend itself. That obstacle is the Supreme Court. This great judicial body is there to guard the prerogatives of the forty-eight States of the Union. And in many vital spheres of public activity and social organization these States are the sovereign power in the country. With us, after centuries of struggle, a central monarchy was formed with a Parliament which devolved power on to the local authorities. The history of the United States of America is exactly the opposite. The thirteen American colonies broke away from England, and became not one country, but thirteen sovereign

States, loosely federated, clinging jealously to their sovereignty, and allowing a weak Federal Government to acquire power only over a few restricted spheres of public activity. Moreover, the American statesmen who founded the Republic were aristocrats and propertied people, who hated democracy. They set up a Constitution which became an instrument for entrenching property rights. The States always were, and still are, the final arbiters on social legislation, wages, hours of employment, social services, public works, and education. If Washington tries to legislate for these matters without the consent of the States, the latter, or any aggrieved citizen, can appeal to the Supreme Court to restrain the Federal Government from infringing its State prerogative and property rights. Government in the United States of America is by diffusion of power, and not by concentration, as with us.

The result of all this is successfully to prevent a democracy, operating by parliamentary majorities, from effecting important social legislation. Here then is the great constitutional issue in America today. It is true that for some time past the natural tendency has been in the direction of more power to the Federal Government. It controls finance, and the States in many cases have little or no financial power; and Washington can demand terms for financial assistance. But in the background is the sinister figure of the Supreme Court, composed of a group of venerable old constitutional lawyers, who regard themselves as the bulwarks of property rights, and of a social order which seemed in the eighteenth century to be unchanging and unchangeable, but which today is an anachronism. Before any serious steps can be taken to implement a popular demand as expressed in the November elections of 1934, this constitutional issue must be decided. And we can be sure that vested interests will use the constitutional lawyers as their chief bulwark.

Meanwhile an unwieldy Democratic majority in Congress will get restive and show signs of breaking up under the intrigues of graft politicians and placemen. Prospects are not bright, but the President impresses one as the type of statesman whom the United States of America has always thrown up in times of crisis. He is the product of the same sort of crisis which threw up Washington and Lincoln. His task is to endeavour to steer American society into the first stage of economic and social planning, while avoiding the constitutional dangers, but if necessary removing them.

As my wife and I left America's shores on December 9, 1934, our last wish, as we saw the floodlit Statue of Liberty disappear in the winter haze of the Hudson, was that the new phase of American history which is now opening shall be as rich in great men and noble achievements as the past phases have been, and that the English-speaking people on both sides of the Atlantic, in view of the dangers to our common liberties from the rise of militarism and Fascist dictators in Europe, shall understand each other as never before. The United States today, to an Englishman, is a most interesting country. Russia has gone through great convulsions, but is now settling down to developments on definite lines. But the United States is on the eve of great changes, and no one knows just how those changes will come, or what will emerge from them.

Indeed the time chosen for our journey was more momentous as regards the future of America, than were the years 1869 and 1878, when my father made his two journeys after the Civil War. Then the wealth of a continent could still be exploited in a wild rush of individual effort. Today, if America is to live, her citizens must learn to co-operate in house-keeping. A beginning has been made, but the way is long and difficult.

GEORGE ALLEN & UNWIN LTD
LONDON: 40 MUSEUM STREET, W.C.1
LEIPZIG: (F. VOLCKMAR) HOSPITALSTR. 10
CAPE TOWN: 73 ST. GEORGE'S STREET
TORONTO: 91 WELLINGTON STREET, WEST
BOMBAY: 15 GRAHAM ROAD, BALLARD ESTATE
WELLINGTON, N.Z.: 8 KINGS CRESCENT, LOWER HUTT
SYDNEY, N.S.W.: AUSTRALIA HOUSE, WYNYARD SQUARE

Foreign Travelers in America
1810–1935

AN ARNO PRESS COLLECTION

Archer, William. **America To-Day**: Observations and Reflections. 1899.

Belloc, Hilaire. **The Contrast.** 1924.

[Boardman, James]. **America, and the Americans.** By a Citizen of the World. 1833.

Bose, Sudhindra. **Fifteen Years in America.** 1920.

Bretherton, C. H. **Midas, Or, The United States and the Future.** 1926.

Bridge, James Howard (Harold Brydges). **Uncle Sam at Home.** 1888.

Brown, Elijah (Alan Raleigh). **The Real America.** 1913.

Combe, George. **Notes on the United States Of North America During a Phrenological Visit in 1838-9-40.** 1841. 2 volumes in one.

D'Estournelles de Constant, Paul H. B. **America and Her Problems.** 1915.

Duhamel, Georges. **America the Menace**: Scenes from the Life of the Future. Translated by Charles Miner Thompson. 1931.

Feiler, Arthur. **America Seen Through German Eyes.** Translated by Margaret Leland Goldsmith. 1928.

Fidler, Isaac. **Observations on Professions, Literature, Manners, and Emigration, in the United States and Canada, Made During a Residence There in 1832.** 1833.

Fitzgerald, William G. (Ignatius Phayre). **Can America Last?** A Survey of the Emigrant Empire from the Wilderness to World-Power Together With Its Claim to "Sovereignty" in the Western Hemisphere from Pole to Pole. 1933.

Gibbs, Philip. **People of Destiny**: Americans As I Saw Them at Home and Abroad. 1920.

Graham, Stephen. **With Poor Immigrants to America.** 1914.

Griffin, Lepel Henry. **The Great Republic.** 1884.

Hall, Basil. **Travels in North America in the Years 1827 and 1828.** 1829. 3 volumes in one.

Hannay, James Owen (George A. Birmingham). **From Dublin to Chicago**: Some Notes on a Tour in America. 1914.

Hardy, Mary (McDowell) Duffus. **Through Cities and Prairie Lands:** Sketches of an American Tour. 1881.

Holmes, Isaac. **An Account of the United States of America,** Derived from Actual Observation, During a Residence of Four Years in That Républic, Including Original Communications. [1823].

Ilf, Ilya and Eugene Petrov. **Little Golden America:** Two Famous Soviet Humorists Survey These United States. Translated by Charles Malamuth. 1937.

Kerr, Lennox. **Back Door Guest.** 1930.

Kipling, Rudyard. **American Notes.** 1899.

Leng, John. **America in 1876:** Pencillings During a Tour in the Centennial Year, With a Chapter on the Aspects of American Life. 1877.

Longworth, Maria Theresa (Yelverton). **Teresina in America.** 1875. 2 volumes in one.

Low, A[lfred] Maurice. **America at Home.** [1908].

Marshall, W[alter] G[ore]. **Through America:** Or, Nine Months in the United States. 1881.

Mitchell, Ronald Elwy. **America:** A Practical Handbook. 1935.

Moehring, Eugene P. **Urban America and the Foreign Traveler, 1815-1855.** With Selected Documents on 19th-Century American Cities. 1974.

Muir, Ramsay. **America the Golden:** An Englishman's Notes and Comparisons. 1927.

Price, M[organ] Philips. **America After Sixty Years:** The Travel Diaries of Two Generations of Englishmen. 1936.

Sala, George Augustus. **America Revisited:** From the Bay of New York to the Gulf of Mexico and from Lake Michigan to the Pacific. 1883. 3rd edition. 2 volumes in one.

Saunders, William. **Through the Light Continent;** Or, the United States in 1877-8. 1879. 2nd edition.

Smith, Frederick [Edwin] (Lord Birkenhead). **My American Visit.** 1918.

Stuart, James. **Three Years in North America.** 1833. 2 volumes in one.

Teeling, William. **American Stew.** 1933.

Vivian, H. Hussey. **Notes of a Tour in America from August 7th to November 17th, 1877.** 1878.

Wagner, Charles. **My Impressions of America.** Translated by Mary Louise Hendee. 1906.

Wells, H. G. **The Future in America:** A Search After Realities. 1906.